22062.

THE MILLENNIUM: CHRISTIANITY AND RUSSIA

The Millennium:
Christianity and Russia
(A.D. 988–1988)

Edited by
Albert Leong

ST VLADIMIR'S SEMINARY PRESS
CRESTWOOD, NY 10707
1990

The Millennium: Christianity and Russia (A.D. 988–1988)
University of Oregon, Eugene, OR.

The millennium project is sponsored by the Oregon Committee for the Humanities (an affiliate of the National Endowment for the Humanities); the University of Oregon Russian and East European Studies Center, Museum of Art, Foundation, Gaston Bequest, Bookstore, Failing Fund, Library, Visiting Scholars Fund, College of Arts and Sciences, Center for the Humanities, Honors College, Alumni Association, Office of the President, School of Architecture and Allied Arts, School of Music, ASUO Cultural Forum, and the Departments of Russian, History, Religious Studies, Art History, Fine and Applied Arts, Architecture, and Art Education; Ashley Foster, Mrs George Kobilkin, Roscoe Divine, Kenneth C. Moore, Time-Life, Inc., and Mrs. Marjorie Lindholm.

Library of Congress Cataloging-in-Publication Data

The Millennium: Christianity and Russia, A.D. 988–1988 / edited by Albert Leong.

    p.   cm.
Includes bibliographical references and index.
ISBN 0–88141–080–2

   1. Christianity—Soviet Union—Congresses. I. Leong, Albert.
BR932.M54 1990
274.7—dc20   90-46791 CIP

Typeset at St Vladimir's Seminary on a Northgate 386/20 PC using Ventura Publisher 3.0 and printed on a QMS PS 810 printer using Adobe Garamond 12pt on 13.5 leading and Laser Cyrillic and Laser SuperGreek Fonts from Linguist's Software.

Table of Contents

Part 2   *Christianity and Russian Culture*

Appendices

Preface: Christianity and Russia

Albert Leong

University of Oregon

I. Oregon and the Millennium

In A.D. 988, according to the *Russian Primary Chronicle (Povest' vremennykh let)*, Grand Prince Vladimir I of Kiev replaced paganism with Eastern Orthodox Christianity as the official religious orientation of Kievan Russia. Throughout the year 1988, the millennium of Christianity in Russia was observed worldwide, including the Soviet Union.

In the fall of 1987 the Russian and East European Studies Center (REESC) of the University of Oregon received a grant from the Oregon Committee for the Humanities to present a public humanities symposium April 10–16, 1988, on "The Millennium: Christianity and Russia (A.D. 988–1988)." Co-directed by Albert Leong, head of the Department of Russian and director of the Russian and East European Studies Center, and A. Dean McKenzie, professor of art history, the Millennium Project at the University of Oregon was designed to give the Oregon community an opportunity to join this worldwide observation and to offer the general public a balanced understanding of the relationship between Christianity and the history and culture of Russia and the Soviet Union.

The unifying theme of the Oregon Millennium Project was the impact of Eastern Orthodox Christianity on the historical and cultural development of Russia and the Soviet Union. The symposium examined, from different perspectives, the meaning of Orthodox Christianity and its influence on the humanities in Russia and the Soviet Union today. The purpose of the symposium was not to achieve a consensus of opinion, but to explore a wide range of positions pertaining to Orthodox Christianity in Russia and the USSR. The program of free lectures, exhibits, films, concerts, and discussions provided the general public with a better understanding of Russian culture and civilization.

The Millennium Project featured four exhibitions integrated with the symposium on Christianity and Russia: "Sacred Images and the Millennium" and "The Empire That Was Russia: A Photographic Record by Sergei Prokudin-Gorsky" at the University of Oregon Museum of Art; "The Russian Orthodox Church: Architecture for a Millennium" in Gallery 141 of the University of Oregon School of Architecture and Allied Arts; and a book exhibit at the University of Oregon Knight Library.

Curated by Professor McKenzie, "Sacred Images and the Millennium" displayed Russian icons dating from the fourteenth to the twentieth century to illustrate traditional themes in Orthodox iconography.

The Prokudin-Gorsky photographic exhibition from the Library of Congress contained rare color images of the Russian Empire under Tsar Nikolai II. Among the most memorable photographs made by Sergei Prokudin-Gorsky were those of Russian churches as they stood before the ravages of the 1917 Russian Revolution. Exquisite and tranquil, these churches and cathedrals recall Holy Russia, when Church and State were one, and the Orthodox faith was the bond and spiritual source that nourished a nation.

"The Russian Orthodox Church: Architecture for a Millennium," consisted of photographs of Russian churches taken by McKenzie and William C. Brumfield (Tulane University), and architectural models of medieval Russian churches made by students of the School of Architecture and Allied Arts.

An exhibit of books on Russian icons and architecture, as well as facsimiles of illuminated liturgical and Biblical texts dealing with Christianity in Russia, was arranged by Howard Robertson of the Knight Library.

These four exhibitions set the stage for the public humanities symposium on "The Millennium: Christianity and Russia (A.D. 988–1988)" during which American scholars of Russian history and culture discussed the impact of the Christianization of Kievan Russia by Prince Vladimir I of Kiev in A.D. 988 on the subsequent historical and cultural development of Russia and the Soviet Union.

The symposium coincided with the celebration of Orthodox Easter, and a program of Orthodox liturgical music for Easter was presented on April 3 by the St. Nicholas Ensemble of Portland, Oregon, under the direction of Dennis Oliver. Josef Gulka and the Kyril-Methodios Ensemble gave a lecture-demonstration on "Christianity and Russian Music" on April 14 and closed the symposium on April 16 with a concert of Russian liturgical music.

The grand opening of the symposium on Sunday, April 10, at the Museum of Art featured a public reception, the opening of the Prokudin-Gorsky and Russian icon exhibitions, and the keynote lecture by Professor Nicholas V. Riasanovsky.

The welcoming remarks by Paul Olum, President of the University of Oregon, Donald Van Houten, Dean of the College of Arts and Sciences, and Wilmot Gilland, Dean of the School of Architecture and Allied Arts, reflected the broad base of university support for the Millennium Project. Of particular significance to the University of Oregon was the participation of three alumni, all of whom later became Rhodes Scholars and specialists on Russian history: Alexander V. Riasanovsky (University of Pennsylvania); Nicholas V. Riasanovsky (University of California, Berkeley); and Donald W. Treadgold (University of Washington). During the symposium, all three scholars were presented with the Webfoot Award for distinguished achievements in the Slavic field at the first annual Recognition Banquet sponsored by the College of Arts and Sciences.

II. Christianity and Russia

The ten papers in this monograph include eight lectures presented at the University of Oregon symposium on "The Millennium: Christianity and Russia (A.D. 988–1988)." This collection is divided into two main parts: (1) Christianity and Russian History and (2) Christianity and Russian Culture. In Part One Alan Kimball's "Introduction: Russia and the Millennium" investigates the role that Ol'ga and Anna played in the conversion of Kievan Russia to Orthodox Christianity. Nicholas V. Riasanovsky's keynote speech, "The Christianization of Russia in Historical Perspective," concisely analyzes the implications of the "decisive historical choice" of Eastern Christianity that the Rus' made in the tenth century. In his essay, "Russia: The Christian Beginnings," George P. Majeska (University of Maryland) documents the military and political motives underlying the alliance between Kievan Russia and Byzantium that led to the baptism of the Rus.

Drawing upon existing Arabic sources, William E. Watson (University of Pennsylvania) describes the Arabic perception of Russia's Christian conversion in light of the formidable military reputation earned by the Rus' in the Near East. In his article on the Ukrainian Church, Basil Dmytryshyn (Portland State University) presents the Ukrainian view of the acceptance of Christianity and traces the subsequent trials and tribulations of the Church. It should be noted, however, that the departure of the Ukrainian Autocephalous Church from the Orthodox and Roman Catholic doctrine of Apostolic succession has impeded its recognition by world Orthodoxy.

Two essays in this collection discuss the fate of Orthodox Christianity in the Soviet Union. Donald W. Treadgold's "Christianity and Russia in the Modern Era" depicts the various forms of suppression practiced against the Orthodox Church by the Bolsheviks following the Revolution of 1917 and the current upsurge of interest in religion in the USSR. Robert L. Nichols' "Dissent and Conformity in the Russian Orthodox Church, 1943-1988" compares and contrasts the persecution experienced by the Orthodox Church during the Stalin era to Gorbachev's current policy of *glasnost'* (openness) and *perestroika* (restructuring) *vis-a-vis* the Russian Orthodox Church.

Part Two (Christianity and Russian Culture) consists of three articles, one on Russian liturgical music and two on Russian religious art. In their collective article, "Problems of Liturgical Abuse in Sixteenth and Seventeenth Century Russia," Josef Gulka (University of Pennsylvania) and Alexander V. Riasanovsky analyze three major areas of abuse or musical distortion in the liturgical practices of the Russian Orthodox Church: *khomoniia; mnogoglasie; anenaika* and *khabuvoe penie.*

In "The Transformation of the Russian Sanctuary Barrier and the Role of Theophanes the Greek," Maria Cheremeteff (California College of Arts and Crafts), delineates the changes undergone by the iconostasis and the contributions made by Theophanes the Greek to this transformation. In "Political Aspects in Russian Icons," A. Dean McKenzie (University of

Oregon) analyzes the political themes and images depicted in Russian icons to shed light on the close relationship between Church and State in Russian cultural history.

In the Appendix the "Catalog of Symposium Audio and Videotapes" compiled by Martha Sherwood-Pike (University of Oregon) lists recordings of symposium presentations and concerts that are available to the public at cost. The symposium on Christianity and Russia was offered for optional credit at the University of Oregon, and schools wishing to present a one-term course on the millennium of Christianity in Russia can do so by ordering a set of symposium videotapes to supplement this book.

Complementing the symposium lectures was a series of documentary and feature films related to the theme of Christianity, Russia, and the millennium. Albert Leong introduced the film version of Modest Musorgskii's opera, *Boris Godunov* (USSR, 1987), two films by the late Soviet Russian filmmaker Andrei Tarkovsky — *Andrei Rublev* (USSR, 1966) and *The Sacrifice* (Sweden, 1986) — and the documentary film *Candle in the Wind* (USA, 1984). Musorgskii's folk drama, based on Aleksandr Pushkin's Shakespearean play inspired by Nikolai Karamzin's *History of the Russian State,* depicts the intricate relation between the Tsar, the Russian Orthodox Church, and the Russian people during the Time of Troubles (1598-1613). The monk-chronicler Pimen, like Nestor in *The Russian Primary Chronicle,* and the Holy Fool *(yurodivy)* in *Boris Godunov* embody profound aspects of Russian Orthodoxy.

In *Andrei Rublev* Tarkovsky created an epic film biography of Russia's greatest icon painter and dramatized the role of the religious artist in Russian society. In *The Sacrifice,* his final film, Tarkovsky dramatized the Russian Orthodox concept of sacrifice and martyrdom in the modern context of nuclear holocaust. *Candle in the Wind,* shown in conjunction with the panel discussion on "Christianity and Russian Culture" at the conclusion of the symposium, is a provocative film essay on the impact of Communism on the practice of Christianity, Judaism, and the Islamic faith in the Soviet Union.

Alan Kimball introduced Sergei Eisenstein's film, *Ivan the Terrible, Part 1* (USSR, 1944), which depicts the conflict between Church and State under Tsar Ivan IV (1530–84), and Richard Morris introduced

Margaret Hixon's documentary film, *Old Believers* (USA, 1981), which records the folkways of the Russian Old Believer community in Marion County, Oregon.

Four other symposium presentations — "New Insights on Old Beliefs," by Robert O. Crummey (University of California, Davis), "Religion and Cultural Antipathy" by Gustave Alef (University of Oregon), "Photographing the Russian Empire: Prokudin-Gorsky" and "The Distinctive Character of Russian Church Architecture" by William C. Brumfield (Tulane University) — are available on tape, but could not be included in this volume.

III. Christianity and Russian Literature

In retrospect, the symposium might have discussed in greater detail the question of how the Christianization of Russia affected the development of Russian literature. Prince Vladimir's acceptance of Eastern Orthodox Christianity in A.D. 988 not only established a political alliance between Kievan Russia and Byzantium, but also created conditions for the birth and flowering of Russian literature and culture. Christianization gave Kievan Russia a written language and, with it, access to the literary treasures of Byzantine culture. Translations of the Bible, sermons, and saints' lives were the first literature that the newly literate Russians assimilated. And these aesthetic experiences shaped the future development of culture in Russia: in the dawn of Russian literature there was the Word, and those Words were sacred.

Thus, most likely, began the tradition of public reverence towards writers and their works that marks the relationship between artist and audience in Russia and, now, in the Soviet Union. The first writers of Russia were learned churchmen such as Nestor *(The Russian Primary Chronicle)*, Ilarion *(Sermon on Law and Grace)*, or Kiril of Turov *(Sermons)*. In the nineteenth century masters of the word such as Aleksandr Pushkin, Nikolai Gogol', Fedor Dostoevskii, and Lev Tolstoi were also expected to uphold the lofty mission of the Russian writer as the voice and conscience of the Russian people — a tradition that continues in the popular veneration of Boris Pasternak, Vladimir Vysotskii, and Aleksandr Solzhenitsyn in the Soviet Union today.

Yet that veneration of lofty edifying literature also produced the distinctive phenomenon of *dvoeverie*, or "double faith," namely the bifurcation of culture into an official one sponsored by the State, and an unofficial underground culture censored and persecuted by the State.

The conversion of the Rus' to Eastern Orthodox Christianity, and the subsequent persecution of paganism, was perhaps the first documented instance of *dvoeverie* in Russian culture. The anonymous *Igor' Tale (Slovo o polku Igoreve)*, a Russian medieval masterpiece attributed to the twelfth century, brilliantly exhibits this dichotomy in its juxtaposition of Christian and pagan elements two hundred years after Prince Vladimir's mass baptism of the Rus' in A.D. 988. It has been noted by literary scholars that the survival of only one copy of the *Igor' Tale* suggests that other copies of this work were destroyed by churchmen due to the predominance of pagan images and themes in the work.

As Robert Nichols and Donald Treadgold note in their essays in this collection, the Bolshevik seizure of power in 1917 drove the Russian Orthodox Church underground as Marxism and atheism were established as the official creed of the Soviet State. The tenuous coexistence of these mutually exclusive ideologies in the Soviet Union remains essentially unchanged, despite Gorbachev's current policies of *glasnost'* and *perestroika*.

It is difficult to imagine Russia or the Soviet Union without the Russian Orthodox Church. Even Stalin needed the Church to inspire Russia and turn the tide of battle in World War II. Indeed, with the present withering of ideological zeal in the USSR, the Soviet State has revived Russian nationalism and once again has turned to the Russian Orthodox Church as a potent source of social, moral, and political stability.

The extraordinary role of the writer in Russia may be a direct result of the unique conditions under which Russia accepted Eastern Christianity in the tenth century. In no other major world civilization does the dawn of culture coincide so clearly with the adoption of a new religious orientation. Because Eastern Christianity, with its synthesis of the arts of poetry, painting, and music in liturgical practice, is a faith that celebrates the unity, harmony, and interconnectedness of all creation, all these arts developed with unusual rapidity in the newly Christianized Kievan State.

Moreover, the harmony of word, music, and sacred image in Orthodox liturgical practice stimulated the development of an aesthetics of synthesis in art that can be seen in the theory and practice of holistic artists such as Andrei Rublev (1370?–1430?), Vasilii Kandinskii (1866–1944), Kazimir Malevich (1878–1935), Vladimir Tatlin (1885–1953), Pavel Filonov (1883–1941), and Ernst Neizvestny (1926–). The articles in this collection by Josef Gulka and Alexander Riasanovsky, Maria Cheremeteff, and Dean McKenzie touch upon the aesthetics of early Russian music and art.

Eastern Christianity and Byzantium also provided an abundance of literary models for the future development of Russian literature. Russian literature, both medieval and modern, has elaborated brilliantly on the ancient Biblical theme of "transgression" and "retribution." The Russian national poet Aleksandr Pushkin (1799–1837) executes subtle variations on this theme: Aleko *(The Gypsies)*, Eugene *(Eugene Onegin)*, Salieri *(Mozart and Salieri)*, Don Juan *(The Stone Guest)*, Germann *(The Queen of Spades)*, and Tsar Boris *(Boris Godunov)* all transgress God's law by taking life in acts of hubris and are doomed to isolation, dementia, or death.

Moreover, in *Boris Godunov* Pushkin creates memorable images of the monk-chronicler Pimen as the objective hand of history unmasking the crimes of Tsar Boris, and of the *yurodivy* ("Holy Fool in Christ") as the martyred conscience of the Russian people. It was Pushkin's narrative poem, *The Bronze Horseman*, that evoked the myth of St. Petersburg as a monument to autocratic will (Peter the Great) and the antithesis of natural law. Aleko, a fugitive from the imperial capital who unwittingly contaminates the natural world of *The Gypsies*, is last seen as a "wounded bird" with nowhere to go. In his *Pushkin Speech*, Dostoevskii describes Aleko as the quintessential "rootless Russian wanderer."

The mature works of Nikolai Gogol' (1809–1852) also dramatize this timeless conflict between good and evil, between God and the Devil. His *Petersburg Tales* are set in the "the Devil's city," where the Devil himself lights the lamps at twilight and casts shadows of illusion on all values and relationships. In *The Overcoat* from this cycle he depicts a humble, saintly scribe, Akakii Akakievich, overwhelmed by the demonic forces of frost, materialism, and spiritual vulgarity *(poshlost')*. His fall is prompted by the tailor Petrovich, whose name ("son of Peter") alludes to the Tsar who was regarded by the Old Believers as the "Anti-Christ" due to his thorough-going westernizing reforms. In his great comedy *The Inspector General,* Gogol' satirizes a town governed by inept officials as Judgment Day arrives in the form of the real government inspector. And, finally, Gogol' wrote *Dead Souls* as an religious allegory patterned after Dante's *Divine Comedy,* with Chichikov undergoing spiritual transformation in Part Two.

Fedor Dostoevskii (1821–81) sustains and deepens the myth of St. Petersburg in his major works. Set in what Dostoevskii considers the most "fantastical" and "premeditated" city, the action of the *Notes from the Underground* affirms absolute free will and moral responsibility by un-masking rationalism, materialism, and scientific determinism with their reductionist view of human personality. In *Crime and Punishment* the nihilist Raskolnikov, true to his name ("schismatic"), cuts himself off from the Russian community by murdering two women with an axe but finds redemption through the Christian humility and compassion of Sonia ("Holy Wisdom"). In *The Idiot* Dostoevskii presents Prince Mysh-kin as a Christ figure martyred in his attempt to defuse the forces of power and violence symbolized by Ragozhin. In the positive characters of Father Zosima and Aleksei Karamazov in *The Brothers Karamazov,* Dostoevskii depicts vigorous proponents of active love in Orthodox practice in his adaptation of the medieval Russian literary genre of the saint's life.

In his *Diary of a Writer* Dostoevskii speaks eloquently about Christ and Russia: "The Russian people know Christ, their God, perhaps even better than we, though they did not study in school. They know Him because for many centuries they have borne many sufferings and in their grief have always, from the beginning until now, heard about this God their Christ from their saints ... The Russian man knows nothing more lofty than Christianity, and cannot imagine anything loftier. He has called his whole land, his whole community, all Russia, 'Christianity' *(Khristianstvo)* and the 'peasantry' *(krestianstvo),* "that is to say, the "cross-bearing people."

It was Dostoevskii who wrote: "Without a higher idea, neither a man nor a nation can exist. But on earth there is *only one* higher idea — namely, the idea of the immortality of the human soul. The fundamental idea underlying Dostoevskii's works from *Crime and Punishment* to *The*

Brothers Karamazov is that "love for humanity is altogether unthinkable, unintelligible, and altogether impossible without concomitant faith in the immortality of the human soul."

Nikolai Leskov (1831–95) celebrated the Orthodox clergy in *Cathedral Folk* and evoked the image of the holy fool in his novellas and short stories. Lev Tolstoi (1828–1910) in his maturity wrote religious parables for children, depicted wise peasants such as Platon Karataev in *War and Peace* as holy fools, and authored a treatise on art *(What Is Art?)* that included religious art along with folk art as the two categories of good art uniting people through intense, sincere shared feelings. Even Ivan Turgenev (1818–83) shows Bazarov, the militant nihilist of *Fathers and Children,* accepting the Orthodox rite of extreme unction before his death. And Anton Chekhov (1860–1904) in late works such as "The Bishop" reconciled his Orthodox heritage with his scientific training as a physician in a warmly sympathetic portrayal of an Orthodox Russian priest.

In twentieth century Russian literature the symbolist poet Aleksandr Blok (1880–1921) dramatized the Revolution of 1917 in "The Twelve" as the Second Coming of Christ. In *Mahogany,* Boris Pil'niak (1894–1937?) glorifies the Trotskyites as holy fools in Bolshevik Russia. In *Doctor Zhivago* by Boris Pasternak (1890–1960), the hero resembles St. George (Yury) taking on the dragon of Bolshevik rule. In his picaresque novel *The Master and Margarita* Mikhail Bulgakov (1891–1940) juxtaposes the master artist with Christ.

And Aleksandr Solzhenitsyn (1918–), uniquely synthesizing the teachings of Dostoevskii and Tolstoi, asserts in his *Nobel Lecture on Literature* that "beauty will save the world" and that "one world of truth will outweigh the whole world." Solzhenitsyn attributes the evils besetting Russia to its repudiation of God, its renunciation of moral responsibility, and its denying the immortality of the human soul, which to Dostoevskii was the one "higher idea" sustaining human life on earth. In "Matryona's Home" Solzhenitsyn characterizes the saintly peasant woman Matryona as "the righteous one, without whom no village can stand." His *One Day in the Life of Ivan Denisovich* depicts the martyrdom of the pious Russian peasantry as "the most profound tragedy of all the tragedies that Russia has endured."

Solzhenitsyn's monumental *Gulag Archipelago* can be compared to Dante's *Divine Comedy* in its tripartite structure corresponding to the *Inferno, Purgatory,* and *Paradise.* As Dante did in *The Divine Comedy,* Solzhenitsyn dwells on the work's allegorical meaning, namely, that "man, as by good or evil use of his free will, merits just reward or renders himself liable to just punishment." In Book Two of the *Gulag Archipelago,* he describes his own rebirth as an Orthodox Christian in a chapter that dramatizes in poetry and prose his loss and restoration of faith in God with Dostoevskian pathos: "A BLESSING TO THEE, PRISON (BLAGO-SLOVENIE TEBE TIUR'MA) for having been in my life! "

This discussion of major writers and works in the history of Russian literature notes the profound impact that Orthodox Christianity had, and continues to have, on the form, substance, and development of Russian literature.

IV. Acknowledgments

My work as co-director of the Oregon Millennium Project, director of the symposium on "The Millennium: Christianity and Russia (A.D. 988–1988)," and editor of this monograph was greatly facilitated by the assistance, encouragement, and cooperation of many individuals at the University of Oregon and in the Eugene community.

First of all, I wish to express my appreciation to my colleagues in the University of Oregon Russian and East European Studies Center, Alan Kimball, A. Dean McKenzie, and Howard Robertson, whose spirit of collegiality, commitment of time, and abundance of ideas made the Oregon Millennium Project a reality. Sue Keene, Acting Director of the Museum of Art, made the facilities of the musuem available for the Russian icon and Prokudin-Gorsky exhibitions, as well as concerts, lectures, and the opening reception.

Kathleen Bowman, Associate Vice-President for Research and Director of the Office of Research and Sponsored Programs at the University of Oregon, and Robert Keeler of the Oregon Committee for the Humanities also contributed to the development of the project.

The Oregon Millennium Project was made possible by support from the Oregon Committee for the Humanities (an affiliate of the National

Endowment for the Humanities); the University of Oregon Foundation, Gaston Bequest, Henry Failing Fund, Bookstore, Knight Library, Instructional Media Center, Office of the Registrar, Visiting Scholars Fund, College of Arts and Sciences, Humanities Center, Robert D. Clark Honors College, Alumni Association, Office of the President, School of Architecture and Allied Arts, School of Music, ASUO Cultural Forum, Russian and East European Studies Center, and the Departments of Russian, History, Religious Studies, Art History, Fine and Applied Arts, Architecture, and Art Education; Ashley Foster, Mrs. George Kobilkin, Roscoe Divine, Kenneth C. Moore, Time-Life, Inc., and Mrs. Marjorie Lindholm. Paul Olum, President of the University of Oregon, and Larry Large, Vice-President for Public Affairs and Development, were instrumental in securing timely funding from the UO Foundation for the icon and photographic exhibitions at the Museum of Art.

Norman Wessells, Provost, and Donald Van Houten, Dean of the College of Arts and Sciences, graciously underwrote the cost of preparing the manuscript and art program of this book for publication by St. Vladimir's Seminary Press.

I wish to express my gratitude to the authors of the manuscripts for their cooperation in preparing and proofing their contributions for publication in this monograph. It was a pleasure to work with such knowledgeable and dedicated colleagues in the Slavic field and to give more permanent form to their insights on the relationship between Christianity and Russia.

Martha Sherwood-Pike, administrative assistant for the project, prepared William Watson's paper for publication and entered the musical notation of the paper by Josef Gulka and Alexander Riasanovsky. Christopher Syrnyk transcribed the tape of Donald Treadgold's lecture and collated it with the written text. He and Sarah McArthur entered the manuscripts into the computer for final editing by me. An earlier gift of a Macintosh workstation from Apple Computer facilitated the development of the Millennium Project and the preparation of this monograph for publication. Roy Singer of the Erb Memorial Union Computer Lounge transferred the text into the IBM format on diskette. I wish to thank Theodore Bazil, Managing Editor of SVS Press, John Meyendorff, Dean of St. Vladimir's Orthodox Seminary, and Glen Mules, Member of the Board of Trustees, for their assistance in bringing this book to press.

The Millennium brochure was designed by Albert Leong, Dean McKenzie, and George Beltran. Both the Millennium poster and brochure were printed by the University of Oregon Printing Department. The catalog to the Russian icon exhibition, *Sacred Images and the Millennium,* was written and published by Dean McKenzie, who also provided the icon illustrations from the exhibition that are used in this book.

Finally, I would like to dedicate this monograph to my wife Annette, whose understanding, support, and wise advice made the Millennium Project and this book possible. My children — Adam, Anna, and Davina — as always are a source of wonderment and inspiration.

As Editor of this monograph, I am responsible for whatever shortcomings this collection may have. Suggestions for subsequent editions of this book are invited and may to addressed to the editor ᶜ/o Department of Russian, University of Oregon, Eugene, Oregon 97403. Telephone: (503) 346-4078.

Part 1
Christianity and Russian History

The Apparition of the Virgin to St. Sergius [Russian, 16C.]
University of Oregon Museum of Art, Eugene, OR

1

Introduction: Russia and the Millennium

Alan Kimball
University of Oregon

In April 1988, the University of Oregon Russian and East European Studies Center (REESC), the Oregon Committee for the Humanities, and dozens of other university departments and private citizens sponsored an extensive public symposium in Eugene, Oregon, devoted to the Millennium of Christianity in Russia. The full commemoration consisted of lectures, panel discussions, exhibits of icons, books, and historical photos of Russia, movies, and a lecture/concert of Slavonic liturgical music. A national committee, which formed in Washington, D.C.—and called itself "Millennium Committee Commemorating 1000 Years of the Christianization of Rus' "—reported that nearly five dozen major commemorations of this anniversary were scheduled all around the world, for example, in Washington, D.C.; Ravenna, Italy; Munich, Germany; Berkeley, California; Moscow, USSR; Paris, France; Kent, England; and, of course, Eugene, Oregon.[1]

Eugene's presence on the list of global centers is unexpected only to those who do not know of the twenty-year history of REESC and its tradition of annual "town-gown" symposia, and the even more venerable tradition represented by the presence on the program and on the pages of this anthology of three distinguished University of Oregon alumni: Alexander and Nicholas Riasanovsky and Donald Treadgold, major figures in the field of Russian history.

Oregon, furthermore, has a special connection with the religious history of Russia. A large settlement of Old-Ritualists is located only a few miles to the north of the university, near Woodburn, Oregon. The ancestors of the Woodburn community fled from the seventeenth-century reforms of Patriarch Nikon and over the centuries have found their way to Oregon variously: via Turkey, China, and South America. The community still seeks religious isolation from certain features of the modern world, and a large contingent from the Oregon community of Old-Ritualists has moved on to Alaska.

Arriving in Alaska, the Old-Ritualists find themselves in very close proximity to Russian Orthodox congregations whose origins are very different from their own. Ranging along the Pacific shores in an arch from the Aleutian Islands to Fort Ross, just above San Francisco, our region is sprinkled over lightly by remnants of Russian imperial power.[2] Perhaps the most lasting legacy of that old empire is Orthodox Christianity. Beginning in the middle of the eighteenth century, tsarist priests, acting as official agents of an expanding empire, originally baptized native settlements along the coasts of Alaska. Many churches still celebrate the Orthodox service, long after tsarist power withdrew from this hemisphere. Thus we see that the millennium of the original Russian baptism, which our symposium commemorated, was followed over the years by a long series of further baptisms at the growing edge of empire. These are processes of both local and global significance.

As I read the papers from the Eugene symposium which have been gathered in this publication, I was reminded of an episode that occurred on a tour taken with my family some time ago to the sites of importance to the history—and present—of the Russian Orthodox Church here in the northwest. We were approached by a priest when we visited the Holy Assumption Orthodox Church in the city of Kenai, on the Kenai Peninsula not far south of Anchorage and only a few miles north of the Old-Ritualist settlements around Nikolaevsk. After introductions and some general conversation, the priest turned to my son and said that he should always remember that Christ's first miracle was performed at Mary's—Jesus' mother's—request when the wine ran out at a wedding reception. The Biblical account suggests that Jesus was hesitant. Mary said to the servants at the wedding, "Do whatever he [Jesus] tells you." Jesus then turned water in large jugs into wine.[3] Always obey your mother, the priest concluded for my son.

I thought of the Orthodox priest's admonition as the Eugene symposium began to raise in my mind the question of the role of women in the Christianization of Russia. History appears in this epoch to have obeyed the commands of women, and our historical accounts do not always do justice to that fact. As never before, in the combined impressions created by George Majeska's and William Watson's essays—both published here—it became clear to me just how central to this whole story were the Grand Princess Ol'ga [Helga] and, later, the Byzantine Princess Anna who became the wife of the Russian Grand Prince Vladimir and perhaps precipitated the event whose millennium is now being observed.

Ol'ga was "wiser than all other men" who had ruled Rus', says the Russian chronicler, and the great nineteenth-century Russian historian S. M. Solov'ev agreed.[4] The Orthodox monks who composed the chronicles remembered Ol'ga fondly because she became a Christian in the Byzantine imperial capital Constantinople in 957 A.D., thirty years before the wedding of Anna and Vladimir. The historian Solov'ev is quick to add that, "as a woman, Ol'ga was more given to domestic affairs, internal matters. Similarly, as a woman, she was especially inclined toward Christianity."[5] A man, by implication, is better suited to the rough and tumble of diplomacy and war, while a woman is more susceptible to Christianity. Yet Solov'ev seems to accept the story which portrays Ol'ga handling herself with dignity and adroitness in the biggest diplomatic league of all: the court of the Byzantine Emperor.

Ol'ga ruled Russia even as her son, the official Grand Prince Sviatoslav, galloped over the land breaking heads with nomadic neighbors. Ol'ga saw beyond the derring-do to the essential problems of trade and administration, the real *Unterbau* of Kievan history. It was with religion, trade, and diplomacy, not warfare, on her mind that she embarked on the perilous journey to Constantinople with an embassy which consisted of nearly two hundred notables, officials, and merchants, not counting military escort. They traveled down the Dnepr River, past the cataracts where fierce nomadic bands often waited in ambush. They crossed the Black Sea (probably hugging the western shore) and arrived at the gates of the great city.

Ol'ga appeared before the Emperor with a retinue of women in the forefront; the men marched in the rear. Constantine sensed the importance of this innovation, so he replicated his initial personal reception with a second in which the Byzantine Empress Elena and her retinue received Ol'ga. Then he scheduled a third reception in which all the Porphyrogeniti met with all the Rus' together in two great halls. Ol'ga's diplomatic delicacy was noted with appreciation.[6]

Ol'ga was "the first woman barbarian ruler ever to behold Byzantium."[7] She had apparently never before pursued a diplomatic initiative of quite this magnitude, nor was such a reception an everyday occurrence in Constantinople.[8] But Ol'ga showed little of her inexperience. Ol'ga understood that this state visit bore heavily on the future of her warrior-merchant principality and on the complex diplomatic and military network which Byzantium maintained. She also had a personal objective, to be baptized. The Emperor sought to help Ol'ga become a Christian, and not against her own inclination. Furthermore—so says the chronicle—he sought a marriage alliance, but in this case not with her full concurrence.

In this connection it was important to the Russian chronicler that Ol'ga "outfoxed" [*perekhitriaet*] the old fox, the Emperor, himself. Ol'ga is made by the chronicler to insist that the Emperor serve as godfather at her christening. Afterward the Emperor renewed his proposal of a marriage alliance. Ol'ga, now christened Elena (after the Empress), reminded him that according to Christian teaching a godfather cannot marry a godchild. The Emperor was forced, in apparent good humor, to withdraw his proposal.[9]

Upon her return to Russia, Ol'ga prayed as Elena, but she ruled as Ol'ga, and her Christianity appears not to have spread among her subjects. It was her grandson, Vladimir, who imposed the faith on the whole realm thirty years after her personal conversion.

But here another woman played a central role, perhaps *the* central role. That woman was Anna, Empress of Byzantium, who became Vladimir's wife in 989. Anna was born in March of 963, six years after Ol'ga's visit and six years before Ol'ga's death. Anna's father, the Emperor Romanus II, died just two days after her birth, leaving her and her older brothers Basil (5 years) and Constantine (2 years) orphans.[10] At the time of her marriage to Vladimir, Anna was thus twenty-six.[11] Her elder sister had already been given in major marriage alliance to Otto, Emperor of the West.[12]

The wedding of Anna and Vladimir is described sometimes as if Anna were little more than movable property, offered in a gentleman's agreement between the Byzantine emperors and the barbarian Prince Vladimir shortly after Vladimir had boldly taken the coastal city Kherson from Byzantium by force.[13] In some accounts she remains unnamed, as if to suggest that this was a simple two-way conversation between the emperors and Vladimir. Evidence suggests that this was not the case at all.

Anna resisted the simple exchange, her troth for her brothers' temporary diplomatic advantage. "I'm being sent as nothing other than a hostage," she is reported to have said. Between the lines one might read that Vladimir had surprised and shaken Anna's brothers; from Kherson he was a real threat to Constantinople. Vladimir sought by swift and unexpected military victory to pressure Constantinople into a hasty and one-sided alliance sealed by marriage. While Basil and Constantine were inclined to accept Vladimir's terms, Anna balked. She apparently took the position that, rather than wed a heathen prince simply to gain a moment's advantage, "it would be better to stay here and die." Anna apparently sought a third alternative, guided perhaps by a strategic grasp of the situation which was superior to that of her brothers. For one thing, she insisted on Vladimir's personal conversion to Christianity. She was also attracted to the possibility that her efforts might bring the whole heathen nation to repentance *[pokaianie]*, i. e., that she might become the agent of Christianization in these northern regions so vital to the strategic position of Byzantium. She was eventually convinced that she could do more than serve as hostage to the pagan prince, and that she need not remain in Constantinople and die. Instead she left for Kherson to meet her groom, with some prospect of the third alternative in her mind.[14]

There is more than a suggestion here that, before Anna's intervention, Vladimir sought something like the opposite of Ol'ga's objectives thirty years earlier. Ol'ga embraced Byzantine Christianity but resisted a marriage alliance with Byzantium. Vladimir sought a marriage alliance, but does not appear to have had a natural inclination toward Christianity. Anna put her foot down.[15] In Kherson—so say the chroniclers—she found Prince Vladimir stricken blind. Anna warned him that his sight would not return if he did not immediately accept baptism. He consented, and, at the story goes, his sight returned immediately. He was convinced beyond any doubt of the wisdom of accepting Christianity. Anna persuaded or compelled Vladimir to become Christian; then she accepted him as husband.[16] That was step one: personal conversion of the prince.

Step two was the conversion of all Rus', and that was a more complex and less documented episode. It did not happen immediately, though we sometimes conflate the personal conversion of Vladimir with the national conversion that followed. Vladimir's personal conversion might have ended the religious story right there in Kherson for the time being; but, after returning to Kiev some time after the personal baptism and wedding, Vladimir embarked on the Christianization of all Rus'.[17] What was first a family drama became a national drama when Vladimir forced all of Rus' to undergo baptism. A contemporary, Ditmar von Walbeck [Thietmar, Bishop of Merseburg], states explicitly that Anna was responsible for this act.[18]

Many factors entered into the conversion of Rus', and we cannot discount the contribution of Anna. Readers will get from George Majeska's essay, published here, a good sense of the long-term growth of Christianity in the decades prior to Anna's marriage to Vladimir, and of the multiple factors that went into that growth. But we cannot escape the sense of historical bump and jolt in this slow process, first with the Kherson wedding and then with the population of Kiev herded into the Dnepr River for baptism. We can well imagine, on the basis of what we know about her character and her later accomplishments, that Anna played a role, not only in the personal conversion of Vladimir, but also in the decision to convert all of Rus'. She was active as adviser to Vladimir and managed considerable lands and a large retinue on her own authority as Princess.[19] Nearly all sources agree that it was largely due to her effort that the construction of the original Christian churches in Kiev got under way.[20]

She, Anna, was not simply a bargaining chip in the dealings between Byzantium and Rus'; she helped decide the fate of her adopted homeland.[21] Anna's daughter, Mariia, extended the tradition of marriage diplomacy when she became the wife of the Polish king Casimir.[22] Anna apparently was the mother of Boris and Gleb, the first great Russian martyred saints.[23] Vladimir supplied the fist behind the Christianization of Rus', but it seems that it was Anna who supplied the will and the spirit. And yet how little credit she receives on the pages of history.[24] As Gibbon remarked so well, "Wolodomir and Anne" are saints of the Russian

Church, "yet we know his vices, and are ignorant of her virtues."[25]

The documentation of this early era is thin and frequently of questionable veracity, so our ignorance of Anna's virtues cannot be fully dispelled, but we still might conclude that the first "miracle" in the history of Christianity in Russia, like Christ's first miracle, was performed in connection with a wedding and at the bidding of a woman. When I say "miracle" I am not speaking of the apocryphal tale of Vladimir's blindness and restoration, but the larger historical process set in motion by the joining of Russia to the main body of European culture, as described in Nicholas Riasanovsky's lead essay in this anthology. Events unfolded from the critical initiatives of women: Ol'ga's diplomatic innovation and Anna's religio-political boldness. We might call Anna the "mother" of Russian Christianization. Nikolai Karamzin conluded that Anna "was an instrument of Heavenly beneficence, who brought Russia out from the darkness of idolatry."[26]

From the earliest beginnings to the most recent events, readers will find in this anthology many surprising and agreeable insights into the history and meaning of Christianity in Russia. George Majeska's informative and thorough account of the Christian beginnings in Rus' and Basil Dmytryshyn's essay on the Ukrainian church provide rich and varied perspectives on what Majeska calls "probably the single most important event in Russian history." For many readers, the most surprising revelations may be the essays by Donald Treadgold and Robert Nichols on the Orthodox Church under Soviet rule. The story of Christianity and Russia begins well before official conversion under Vladimir, and it runs well after official rejection under the Communist Party of the Soviet Union.

The symposium, and most fortunately this anthology as well, emphasize the significance and beauty of the iconographic tradition and the grandeur of Orthodox architecture, such that Anna first brought to Kiev. Maria Cheremeteff on the iconostasis and Dean McKenzie on icons and politics add depth and visual dimension to the historical accounts.[27]

The Orthodox liturgy is dramatic and beautiful, the last great achievement of the classical Greek genius for theater, a spectacle which joins high tragic drama with grand opera and, for the faithful, spiritual *katharsis* and the promise of salvation. A good part of that beauty could not be brought to these pages. Furthermore, given the scholarly mission of the symposium and of our anthology, no explicit effort has been made to bring to these pages the purely devotional elements of Orthodoxy. These elements, nonetheless, are the central meaning of the faith, the church, and the liturgy for those who are communicants in it. Those who attended the Oregon symposium heard the Kyril-Methodios Ensemble and thus had greater access to the beauty of the service, and greater exposure to the liturgy as liturgy, than is possible in the printed medium. Josef Gulka, the director of the ensemble, and Alexander Riasanovsky supply an essay on the liturgy which helps us over that loss. And while the believing Russian Orthodox Christian might deplore our secular approach, it is abundantly clear on every page of this anthology that the Church is not simply a museum of historical antiquities, it is not merely a gallery of beautiful artifacts. For that reason the symposium and this anthology can be called balanced, because the old-fashioned Social-Democrat might deplore our approach every bit as much as the true believer. Furthermore, for a week in Eugene in April, 1988, all parties were equally moved by the magnificence of the great human achievement presented by Russian Orthodoxy. Now a central part of that experience is gathered here in this anthology.

Having passed from wine and women to song, this introduction may now give way to the essays that follow.

NOTES

1. The Millennium Committee, Professor Helen Yakobson, Chairman (George Washington University, Washington, D.C.), *Millennium Newsletter,* no. 2 (November 1987) and no. 3 (March1988).

2. The Oregon Historical Society has published a series on Russia in the New World. See, for example, Basil Dmytryshyn, E. A. P. Crownhart-Vaughan, and Thomas Vaughan, eds. *Russia's Conquest of Siberia, 1558–1700: A Documentary Record.* Vol. 1 of three under the general title "To Siberian and Russian America: Three Centuries of Russian Eastward Expansion, 1558-1867." Oregon Historical Society Series: North Pacific Studies, vol. 9 [–11]. Portland, OR: 1985.

3. John, 2: 1–11.

4. S. M. Solov'ev, *Istoriia Rossii s drevneishikh vremen v piatnadtsati knigakh* (Moscow: 1959), vol. 1, p. 156. For a translation of the chronicle, see Samuel H. Cross and O. P. Sherbowitz-Wetzor, eds., *The Russian Primary Chronicle: Laurentian Text* (Cambridge, MA: 1953), p. 111.

5. Solov'ev, 1:157.

6. The Emperor Constantinus VII Porphyrogenitus, *Emperor of the East,* has left a detailed description of her visit: *De ceremoniis aulae byzantinae..*, vol. 1 (Bonn: 1824), pp. 594–98. A description of the visit in English may be found in Arnold Toynbee, *Constantine Porghyrogenitus and His World* (London: 1973), pp. 504-6. S. D. Skazkin, *et al., Istoriia vizantii v trekh tomakh* (Moscow: 1967), vol. 2, p. 232, says that one half of Ol'ga's suite was made up of merchants. Apparently Skazkin and company did not count the women, since the statistic "one half" can be derived only from Constantine's account of how many men were with Ol'ga and her women: Just over forty of the eighty-plus men in Ol'ga's party were merchants.

7. Charles Diehl, *Byzantium: Greatness and Decline* (New Brunswick, NJ: 1957), p. 57.

8. George Ostrogorsky, *History of the Byzantine State* (New Brunswick, NJ: 1969), p. 382, considers Ol'ga's visit a very significant diplomatic moment.

9. For a translation of the chronicle account, see Serge Zenkovsky, ed., *The Nikonian Chronicle* (Princeton, NJ: 1984), vol. 1, pp. 55–56. See also Cross: 82.

10. Skazkin, 2:211.

11. Sigfus Blondal says Anna was "a mature spinster," *The Varangians of Byzantium,* translated, revised and rewritten by Benedikt S. Benedikz (Cambridge, England: 1978), p. 44.

12. These two royal sisters caught the attention of the famous historian Edward Gibbon. Gibbon describes how, after Otto's death, Anna's sister ruled as regent in the restored Western Empire in Rome, Italy, and Germany. Gibbon devotes particular attention to the marriage or nuptial diplomacy of the Byzantine Empire in these years, particularly as it related to barbarian disorder in the territories north of Constantinople, *The Decline and Fall of the Roman Empire* (New York: Modern Library, *n.d.*), vol.3, pp. 281–4 & 316.

13. See A. A. Vasiliev, in his celebrated *History of the Byzantine Empire, 324-1453* (Madison, WI: 1961), vol. 1, p. 323; and Norman Baynes and H. Moss, *Byzantium: An Introduction to East Roman Civilization* (Oxford, 1948), p.357. Joseph Fuhrmann says that Anna was "sacrificed on the altar of political necessity" ["Anna of Byzantium," *Modern Encyclopedia of Russian and Soviet History,* vol. 2, pp. 7–8].

14. Solov'ev, 1:183. English translations of the chronicle accounts can be found in Cross:111 ff. and Zenkovsky, 1:99-102. V. N. Tatishchev doubted Anna's real historical identity, but he followed Nestor's chronicle account of the nuptial negotiations, placing main accent on Anna's misery and reluctance [*Istoriia rossiiskaia,* 7 volumes (Moscow-Leningrad: 1962-1968), vol. 2, pp. 61 & 227]. Nikolai Karamzin refuted Tatishchev's views on Anna's historical identity, but conceded that it was a puzzle [*Istoriia gosudarstva Rossiiskogo,* 12 volumes, 5th edition (Saint Petersburg: 1842–1843), plus *Kliuch ili alfavitnyi ukazatel' k*

Istorii gosudarstva Rossiskogo N. M. Karamzina, P. Stroev, ed., with "Dvadtsat' chetyre sostavlennye Karamzinym i Stroevym rodoslovnye tablitsy kniazei rossiiskikh" (1844), vol. 1, pp. xv, 130-31 & footnote 464].

15. Gibbon has the argument just about right: "the conversion of Wolodomir was determined, or hastened, by his desire of Roman bride" [Gibbon, 3:341].

16. Ibn al-Athir says that Anna refused the wedding alliance until and unless the Rus' king converted to Christianity. This story is suggested in the Russian chronicles and is corroborated in the sources cited in William Watson's account of Arabic perceptions of the Russian conversion. Watson has augmented V. R. Rozen's insightful analysis of Arabic sources published over one century ago, *Imperator Vasilii Bolgaroboitsa: izvlecheniia iz letopisi Iakh"i Antiokhiiskogo* (Saint Petersburg, 1883) [Variorum reprints, with introduction by Marius Canard (London, 1972)], see especially pp. 217 & 224. I have followed Rozen's interpretation of Vladimir's capture of Kherson (pp. 216-17). I have also been emboldened in my reading between the lines of these accounts by Rozen's insistence: "Nuzhno tol'ko chitat' *mezhdu strok*"(p. 219).

17. M. V. Levchenko, *Ocherki po istorii russko-vizantiiskikh otnoshenii* (Moscow: 1956), p. 364. Anna was the sixth wife of Vladimir. He had about a dozen children by the earlier marriages. One of Anna's first jobs back in Kiev was to convert Vladimir's children. See Tatishchev, 2:61-2; and *Russkii biograficheskii slovar'*, vol. 2, pp. 154-5 [hereafter: RBS].

18. Thietmari Merseburgensis Episcopi, *Chronicon* (Berlin: 1962), p. 432. Anna receives credit: "christianitatis sanctae fidem eius ortatu suscepit." Vladimir is accused of being nothing more than a "fornicator immensus."

19. Shul'gin, V. Ia., *O sostoianii zhenshchiny v Rossii do Petra Velikogo* (Kiev, 1850); Solov'ev, 1:287.

20. Levchenko:365. For deviations from this view, cf. Dimitri Obolensky who gives exclusive credit to Basil II for sending clerics to Russia and refers to "Byzantine architects" who built the first stone church in Kiev *[Byzantium and the Slavs: Collected Studies* (London: 1971), sect. VI, p. 24]. B. D. Grekov gives credit here, not to Basil or Byzantine architects, but to Vladimir, who "was concerned to build churches to give Rus' the appearance of Christianity" *[Kiev Rus'* (Moscow: Foreign Language Publishing House, 1959), p. 498]. Neither Obolensky nor Grekov mentions Anna in this connection.

21. Anna was also responsible for a certain amount of reciprocal Rus' influence back on the Byzantine Empire. Anna sought to maintain and strengthen ties between her adopted homeland, Rus', and her motherland, Byzantium. She dispatched a retinue of Rus' warriors to serve at the side of her brother Constantine. Skazkin, 2:348.

22. *RBS*, 2:154-5. That tradition was yet further extended when in 1051 the great-granddaughter of Anna, the daughter of Yaroslav, became the wife of Henry I. This was the well-educated princess who signed the nuptial vows in

Cyrillic and Latin script while the Frenchman scrawled his illiterate "X." George Majeska relates this story in his essay published in this anthology.

23. Solov'ev, 1:321; and *RBS,* 3:235. Fuhrmann:8 says that "Russian sources are silent concerning Anna's life and role at Kiev. She died there in 1011, apparently bearing Vladimir no children."

24. *Sovietskaia istoricheskaia entsiklopediia* has an article on Ol'ga, but none on Anna. *Entsiklopedicheskii slovar'* (Brokgauz-Efron) also has no separate article on Anna.

25. Gibbon, 3:284. In all likelihood Gibbon was referring here to Walbeck's account, which is so hostile to Vladimir.

26. Karamzin,1:138. Anna did more than bring Christianity to Russia, she also gave Russian rulers their first real claim to imperial descent. Some early documents [see, e.g., Tatishchev, 2:70] refer to Anna as "tsaritsa" (wife of a Caesar). Patriotic tradition in Russian historiography seeks to employ the solid fulcrum of Anna's pedigree, heightened by these terminological slips in the documentation, to lever Vladimir to a higher title—"tsar"—than history was ready yet to grant the Russian princes [e.g., Levchenko:367]. The memory of the union of Byzantium and Russia, through Anna, was important also in Byzantium; it guided a future Byzantine Emperor Manuel to give his son John to the granddaughter of Dmitrii Donskoi, also named Anna [Karamzin, 5:130]. By the time of Ivan IV, the descent of the Russian tsars from the purple of Anna had become stock in trade of Muscovite pride and pretense [Karamzin, 8:58].

27. Readers who would like to learn more of the exhibit which accompanied the Symposium should see the University of Oregon Museum of Art catalogue, *Sacred Images and the Millennium: Christianity and Russia (A. D. 988–1988)* (Eugene, OR: 1988), authored and published by A. Dean McKenzie.

2

The Christianization of Russia in Historical Perspective

Nicholas V. Riasanovsky

University of California, Berkeley

The baptism of the Rus, most probably in 988 A.D., and most probably in or near Kiev, is one of the defining dates in world history. In a famous account, the *Primary Chronicle* narrates how the Rus selected Christianity over Islam and Judaism and, within Christianity, the Byzantine rather than the Roman variant. The point is that, whatever the authenticity of the particular story, the Rus did make, in fact, a decisive historical choice. Great Moslem states and centers of culture lay to the southeast, and Islam was to be a historical factor on the Russian plain itself, ranging from its adoption by the Volga Bulgars to the centuries of the Mongol yoke and the Golden Horde, and to the state of the Crimean Tartars, and beyond. Even Judaism might have been a feasible alternative. At any rate, the Khazar state, which covered the vast territory north of the Caucasus and along the lower Volga, played a major role at the dawn of Kievan history and during its early part, and, in fact, the Khazars might have founded Kiev itself. In other words, Saint Vladimir and his associates chose to become the eastern flank of Christendom rather than an extension into Europe of non-Christian civilizations.

As to the selection of the Byzantine rather than the Roman jurisdiction, the significance might have been less obvious at the time because the two formed parts of the same church. The separation came only in 1054 and, as Professor Francis Dvornik and other scholars have demonstrated, appeared then to be only one more quarrel and at most a temporary break when it happened. Eventually, however, the Catholic-Orthodox divide became one of the main lines of demarcation of Eastern Europe, central to such historical phenomena as the hostility between the Russians and the Poles, and the Ukrainian decision to associate Ukraine with Moscow in 1654.

What followed for the East Slavs, the Great Russians, usually referred to simply as Russians, the Ukrainians and the Belorussians, was the medieval, or quasi-medieval period of their history, with the Church occupying the central role. *Mutatis mutandis*, Orthodox Christendom can be approximately compared to Latin Christendom in terms of its religion, thought, ethical and legal norms, and in terms of the enormous role of the Church in culture, social life, and even politics. Moreover, this quasi-medieval period lasted a long time, in the case of Muscovy until around 1700 and the reforms of Peter the Great.

To be sure, there were major differences between the East and the West. Although the East Slavs after the conversion started with the richest intellectual heritage in all Christendom, the Greek and Byzantine heritage, they did not develop that heritage for a variety of reasons, including the relative paucity of the knowledge of Greek among the Slavs, where Christianity was practiced in Slavonic, while they remained separated from the Latin branch of Christianity with its scholasticism, and other very important late medieval developments. Beyond that, the East Slavs were to miss the Renaissance, the Reformation, and the Counter-Reformation, so important for Central and West European history. The Russians missed these epochal developments completely, The Ukrainians and the Belorussians, much more open to the West, had some part in them as they manifested themselves in the Polish-Lithuanian state. From 1596 on, there arose the so-called Uniate church, a Catholic jurisdiction, which eventually divided the Ukrainians religiously into two major groups, the Orthodox and the Uniate Catholics, the situation that obtains to this day. The Uniates, to be sure, are Christians of the Eastern Rite and, thus, also heirs to the baptism of the Rus in 988.

Short on theology and philosophy, Muscovite Christianity has been justly admired for its visual achievements, the icon painting, the churches, the church ritual itself. Revealingly, the one great break in the Muscovite church occurred in the second half of the seventeenth century when the so-called Old Believers refused to accept even minor corrections and changes in religious practice. The Old Believers have been praised by some as the truest Muscovite Russians, but it is also worth noting that their cause lost in Muscovy and that the Church opted for a certain modernization.

Quasi-medieval Muscovite Russia headed by the tsar and the patriarch (from 1589) and centered on the Church, came to its end with Peter the Great's modernization and secularization. The Spiritual Reglament and other related measures, very much a part of the first emperor's Westernizing reforms, abolished the patriarchate and established the Holy Synod to head a state church, much like other state churches in Lutheran or Anglican Europe. Theologically, and religiously, there was no change, but in political, social, and cultural fact, the change was enormous, all the more so because it reflected a still larger transformation, namely, the gradual transition of educated Russia from a quasi-medieval to a modern secular society. The Russian Church thus continued to function on one level as a "department" of the state, and to offer its support to the empire of the Romanovs. Intellectually and culturally, as in the rest of Europe, religion faded into the background. Religious interests, of course, did not disappear entirely, even among the educated, an obvious point in the case of Dostoevsky and some other creative intellectuals. Moreover, religion, as in 988, still linked Russia to Europe. Until the appearance of an idiosyncratic group who proclaimed themselves in 1921 to be Eurasians, all Russian ideologies accepted this closeness to Europe, with religion often one of its main elements. Thus, the Slavophile Aleksei Khomiakov believed that the crucial break between the West and the East came when the dogma of *filioque* entered the Catholic church without any consultation with the Orthodox brothers. Vladimir Solov'ev (1853–1900) and some other Russian thinkers also explored, at times brilliantly, this fraternal, yet frequently difficult and painful relationship between the East and the West. In fact, the last decades of imperial Russia witnessed the glorious Silver Age in culture, a central part of which was a great revival of independent and varied religious thought.

Then came the Communist Revolution of 1917. In terms of religion, it meant the introduction of atheism as an absolute dogma, and one of the most murderous religious persecutions of modern history. Yet, religion survived, as indicated by the suppressed census of 1936 and much other evidence. In fact, the state came to a certain compromise with the Church, which refused to disappear, assigning to it after the reestablishment of the patriarchate in 1943, a strictly circumscribed role within the Soviet system. The present changes in the Soviet Union may conceivably open new religious vistas. The beginning of the second Millennium of Christianity in Russia is an interesting and important period.

3

Russia: The Christian Beginnings

George P. Majeska
University of Maryland

Always present to the historian discussing the "beginnings" of something is the strong temptation to trace these beginnings from Adam, or from prehistory, depending on his theological outlook. The Greek colonies in South Russia and the Crimea would be the logical Adam from which to trace Christianity in Rus', inasmuch as Christianity in this region is attested from the third century onward in archeological remains and in the historical sources. Unfortunately for the salvation of Slavic peoples north of these Greek colonies, however, regular direct contact with the Christian north coast of the Black sea was impossible. Between the Rus', or their ancestors, and their potential Christian enlighteners stretched a semi-nomadic *cordon sanitaire,* an iron curtain, if you will the successive Steppe empires of western Eurasia. It is not until one of these Steppe empires, the Goths, adopts Christianity in the early fourth century that one might expect to find some representatives of the subject East Slavic peoples following the lead of their conquerors. But while it is possible that some proto-Rus' did indeed learn of Christ from their Christian Gothic overlords, no sources mention it. As a matter of fact, nothing definite is known of the progress of Christianity among the Rus' until the last half of the ninth century, with the exception of the conversion of a certain Rus' prince, Bravlin, in the early part of that century. (Bravlin's case was unique: According to an appendix to the "Life of St. Stephen of Sugdaea," after looting the shrine of St. Stephen during a pirate raid, Bravlin suddenly discovered that his head had been turned backward. On the advice of clerics, Bravlin accepted baptism to be cured of his strange malady. The cure was successful.)

The story of the conversion of the Rus' nation to Christianity is intimately connected with a series of military encounters between the pagan Rus' and the Christian Byzantines. The first military step leading toward eventual conversion was a Rus' attack on Constantinople itself in the year 860. While the attack was repulsed by the speedy return of the Byzantine emperor and his army from a campaign, things had looked so bleak to the inhabitants of the Byzantine capital during the Rus' siege that the victory of the Christian empire over the barbarian Rus' was ascribed to the intervention of the Mother of God. The unexpected appearance of the Rus' barbarian horde before the walls of the "City protected by God" provoked traditional responses on the part of Byzantine policy makers: an attempt to convert and consequently ally with the Rus' or, the other alternative, an attempt to convert and ally with a counter-balancing force in Northeast Europe.

One man, Constantine the Philosopher, known to later history as St. Cyril (he and his brother Methodius are normally spoken of together as the "Apostles of the Slavs"), was entrusted with trying to implement at least one of these policies. In late 860 Constantine left Constantinople with an embassy and proceeded to the Greek city of Kherson in the Crimea. After wintering there and learning Hebrew, by now the lingua franca of the Turkic Khazars ;of the steppe, Byzantium's potential ally against the Rus', Constantine and his party continued on to the Khazar capital. Constantine's preaching and disputation with the Jewish rabbis at the Khazar court produced few converts, but it did produce the sought after Khazar-Byzantine political alliance against the common Rus' enemy.

It is quite possible that, during his year-long stay on the north coast of the Black Sea, Constantine approached the Rus' as well as the Khazars. The Slavonic "Life of St. Constantine," our best source for the Khazar mission, suggests Constantine's interest in the Rus' by noting that while he was in Kherson Constantine showed a serious interest in a Gospel and Psalter written in "Russian letters" (whatever they were, since a Slavic alphabet was apparently not invented until later), and a man who could read them. This brief note by Constantine's biographer might disclose why Constantine was chosen to implement Byzantium's diplomatic and religious policies among the Empire's northern neighbors. Since Constantine did not know Hebrew, the appropriate language for negotiations with the Khazars, possibly he was sent to the north because of his knowledge of Slavic. Slavic would allow the diplomat-missionary to deal directly with the Rus', whose earlier attack on Byzantium was, after all, the basic reason Constantine's mission was undertaken. Later events, as a matter of fact, suggest that Constantine did make contact with the Rus' on the north coast of the Black Sea. For, five years after Constantine's return to the Byzantine capital, that is, in 867, Patriarch Photius of Constantinople boasts in an encyclical that "the Godless Rus' who had wreaked such havoc on the Bosporus just seven years before had accepted Christianity and that a bishop had been dispatched to them. Here we have the first mention of a bishop for the Rus'.

Although Photius does not specify which "Godless Rus'" had moved towards Christianity and friendship with the Empire, it is quite possible that it was the Tmutrokan Rus' whom Constantine could have visited, rather than the better-known group of "Godless Rus'" centered in Kiev. Support for the position that Photius had in mind the Rus' of the tiny and little-known principality of Tmutrokan comes from the fact that Tmutrokan is mentioned in a list of potential missionary centers apparently suggested to Patriarch Photius by Constantine. Since between the years 934 and 976 Tmutrokan was raised to the dignity of an archdiocese, the see must have existed as a simple diocese before this time. Possibly it had been founded at Constantine's suggestion. There is, however, no way of knowing if this diocese had been erected to serve Slavs, Greek colonists, Goths in the area, or as a general missionary center. In any case, a "Bishop of Rus'" is not attested in any sources between the issuing of Photius's encyclical and the official Christianization of Kievan Rus' around the year 988. If making Rus' converts was the aim of the Tmutrokan diocese, it could not have been sufficiently successful to warrant a "Bishop of the Rus'" for any length of time.

The history of the Christian beginnings of Rus' continues to revolve around Rus' attacks on Byzantine cities. We have just noted that the Rus' attack on Constantinople in 860 led to the first religious mission to the Rus'. The treaty signed after the next Rus' attack on Constantinople, in 907, informs us of further missionary opportunities taken by the Byzantine Church. At the conclusion of the treaty, which gave special treatment to Rus' living permanently in Constantinople, a potential source of converts, the *Primary Chronicle,* the basic source for early Rus' history, reports that the Byzantine officials displayed to the Rus' legates the holy relics preserved in Constantinople, and instructed them in the "faith of the Greeks."

The spiritual treasures of Byzantium must have impressed certain of the Rus' at least, for the subsequent Russo-Byzantine treaty, signed in 945, after a particularly unsuccessful Rus' attack on Constantinople, mentions "Christian Rus'" several times. As a matter of fact, Christian Rus' are among the negotiators of the treaty. While some of the Rus' officials subscribe to the treaty in the traditional manner, swearing by their swords and by Perun, the Slavic thunder God, others retire for their oaths to the Christian Church of St. Elias in Kiev itself. Christianity was obviously taking root among the notables of Kiev.

Ten years later, in spite of an extraordinarily un-Christian early widowhood, full of typical Viking cruelty, Ol'ga, regent of the child prince of Kievan Rus', accepted baptism. Her conversion, which eventually led to her veneration as St. Ol'ga, was a personal action, however, not state policy. Her young son Sviatoslav would have none of his mother's civilized religion, claiming that his followers (doubtless his personal retinue of Viking warriors) would laugh at him. The sort of free-booting Norsemen who joined Sviatoslav's raids on the Khazars, Pechenegs, Bulgarians, and Byzantines once the young prince had reached maturity, were, in fact, rather unlikely candidates for the Christian faith, and it is not surprising that not a single Christian Rus' is to be found among the signers of Sviatoslav's 971 treaty with the Byzantines. But even under fiercely pagan Sviatoslav people were not prevented from adopting Christianity, notes the Rus' chronicler, they were merely mocked for it.

Vladimir, the eventual successor to Sviatoslav, was a Viking of truly epic proportions. His ascension to the Kievan throne involved him in the murder of his half-brother. His lust for women was phenomenal, even for a Viking brigand, or so the Rus' chronicler would lead us to believe, possibly exaggerating Vladimir's vices as a pagan in order to point up the great change wrought in the Rus' ruler by his conversion. Besides his cosmopolitan harem of five wives of four different nationalities, Vladimir kept bevies of two or three hundred concubines in three different suburban palaces. As the chronicler aptly remarks, he was a "libertine like Solomon." A later Polish chronicler put the idea more colorfully when he talked of Vladimir as a "*fornicator immensus.*" What better candidate for sainthood than a really solid sinner, and such was young Vladimir, later to be known as "St. Vladimir," the Christianizer of Rus'.

Vladimir's first religious act as leader of Kievan Rus' was not, however, Christianization of the land. Just the opposite: Vladimir established a unified pagan cult for the nation, a cult which included deities revered among the various ethnic groups under Vladimir's sway: Norse, Slavic, Finnish, Lithuanian, and Iranian. This international pantheon must have been rather popular among the masses in Rus', for it is recorded that a Christian Viking was killed by an indignant Kievan mob when he refused his son as a human sacrifice to the idols, thus giving the tiny church in Rus' her first recorded martyr.

In spite of the apparent popularity of pagan worship suggested by the mob reaction in the case just noted, Vladimir's pagan polytheism did not seem to serve the prince's purposes well enough. Paganism, no matter how sophisticated, did not win a nation international respect in the Middle Ages. Thus, after he had rid himself of the undisciplined Viking mercenaries he had hired in Sweden to help him win the Kievan throne, doubtless strong pagans, Vladimir began to consider adopting one of the more respectable religions of the period.

The chronicle recounts, in what must be called a "mythic form," Vladimir's inquiries about the various civilized religions available. The tale of the "trying of the faiths" by Vladimir preserved in the Russian chronicle certainly reflects, in the language of myth, the fact that various religious options were open to the Kievan prince. While it is unlikely that representatives of Islam, Judaism, Western Christianity, and Eastern Christianity came one by one to preach their faith and customs before the ruler of Rus', as the chronicle recounts, by this time all of these faiths were in fact quite familiar to the Rus' from their neighbors. Arabic sources confirm, for instance, that Islam, at least, was seriously considered at the Russian court. Yet while the drawn-out trope of the "trying of the faiths" accurately reflects the religiously unaligned position of the ruler of Kievan Rus', many of the details of the chronicle account of Vladimir's theological investigations are traceable to written tradition available to late editors of the chronicles. Greek and Bulgarian writings and later anti-Latin polemics incorporated into the chronicle are responsible for most of the extraneous details and blatant anachronisms present in the chronicle's story of Vladimir's examination of the different religions. Recorded, although buried in the pages of chronicle rhetoric, is the basic fact that Vladimir chose Byzantine Christianity and Byzantine culture for his realm. The literary rather than historical nature of the chronicle account of Vladimir's investigation of the great religions is demonstrated by Vladimir's reported reason for choosing the "Greek religion." According to the chronicle he chose the "Greek religion" because his envoys to Byzantium were so impressed by the beauty of the liturgy celebrated in Constantinople's Cathedral of St. Sophia that they "knew not whether they were in heaven or on earth. For on earth is not such splendor and beauty." Even the pious chronicler felt constrained to add what to him seemed a more reasonable explanation for the prince's choice: if the "Greek faith" were evil, Vladimir's wise grandmother Ol'ga would not have adopted it. For the circumstances of Vladimir's actual conversion we are not, however, wholly dependent on the Russian chronicle. Other available material—Russian, Greek, and Syriac—places this great event in Russia's history in wider context.

Drawing on contemporary sources other than the chronicle, the following picture emerges: In 987 Emperor Basil II of Byzantium found himself in so precarious a military position vis-à-vis a revolt led by Bardas Phocas that he was forced to cast about for immediate military aid. Prince Vladimir of Kiev seemed the most practical source for such aid, and, actually, Vladimir seemed quite ready to relieve himself of six thousand trained Viking warriors whom he had used to establish his control over Rus', but who had become potential trouble-makers once he was firmly established on the throne of Kiev.

The market set the price high for Vladimir's Vikings. However, because Basil felt that his throne depended on additional forces to be used in the next year's campaign against the insurgents, the Emperor of Byzantium agreed to pay the price—in this case his imperial sister Anna, born in the purple. While the Byzantines had developed an extensive and very useful system of marriage-sealed alliances, a princess born in the sacred palace while her father ruled held a very special place in this system. Such a princess, a *porphyrogenita* (born of the imperial purple) was so intimately connected with the sacred person of the emperor that she was never allowed to marry a foreign ruler. How difficult times had become for Basil is suggested by the fact that twenty years before, the same *porphyrogenita* princess's hand now offered to Vladimir had been refused to the future Emperor Otto II of the Holy Roman Empire. For all the imperial pretensions of the Ottonian empire, the junior Otto was quite content to receive as his bride Theophano, a mere niece of the emperor. As part of the price he had to pay for joining the imperial hierarchy of states on so high a level, son-in-law of the Byzantine Emperor, the secular vicar of Christ on earth, Vladimir was of course required to accept baptism, something he had already decided to do for more intellectually respectable motives, if we accept the kernel of the chronicle account of the "trying of the faiths." Eternal salvation and high rank among the rulers of the civilized world in exchange for six thousand troublesome soldiers is thus the bargain which precipitated the Christianization of Russia.

Not only did Vladimir's Vikings enable the emperor to put down the revolt in the Byzantine empire, but Vladimir himself aided his brother-in-law-elect's war effort by besieging the important Byzantine city of Kherson on the Crimean coast of the Black Sea. It had apparently gone over to the rebels, but Vladimir's new (and still potential) imperial family ties seem to have won over imperial loyalists in the rebellious city. They betrayed the city to him in 989.

The *Russian Chronicle*, which knows nothing of the earlier negotiations for Anna, has Vladimir capturing Kherson and sending a message to the Emperor: "Behold, I have captured your glorious city. I have also heard that you have an unwedded sister"—a rather charming simplification of some very astute political maneuvering.

In any case, Anna was prevailed upon to accept her northern exile for the good of the Empire and of the Church. Vladimir having been baptised (either previously in Kiev or in Kherson after Anna's arrival—the sources on this point are contradictory), the marriage was celebrated in Kherson, and Christianity became the official religion of Rus'. Vladimir returned the city of Kherson to his new imperial father-in-law (as a wedding present, suggests the *Russian Chronicle)* and taking clergy, church vessels, and relics with him, he and his imperial bride returned to Christianize his kingdom.

The idols which Vladimir had once set up in Kiev as a national pantheon were torn down to the accompaniment of great weeping on the part of the populace. But these same people, at least if we accept the testimony of the pro-Christian Rus' chronicler, wept with joy when they were ordered to repair to the river Dnepr to be baptised en masse! Similar scenes were repeated in the other cities of Kievan Rus', apparently also accompanied by something less than joy.

Active opposition to the new religion seems to have been quite rare in the cities of Rus'. The lack of an organized pagan priesthood and the tolerance of the Rus' national religion for foreign deities probably explain the rather peaceful acceptance of the new faith. Slavic paganism seems to have been willing to adopt some traits of Christianity into its practices, as it had earlier adopted elements from the religions of neighboring peoples. Anti-Christian uprisings did come, and were, in fact, serious enough to be responsible for a whole series of martyred missionaries, but they came later, and were largely restricted to cities like Rostov and Novgorod, which had large non-Slavic populations and a strong pagan priesthood.

Baptism was, of course, but the first step in Christianizing the country. To make the new religion effective in Rus' a string of mission stations had to be set up around the country. Such missions must have been organized quickly and efficiently, for by 991 Rus' had its own Metropolitan, and a local hierarchy had been set up, part of the Patriarchate of Constantinople. It seems quite likely that this jurisdictional arrangement was not completely to Vladimir's liking. Doubtless aware that a century earlier Bulgaria had obtained, if only for a short period of time, a hierarchy independent of Constantinople, Vladimir probably attempted to repeat the Bulgarian experiment by following the tried Bulgarian tactics: playing the western part of the Church against the See of Constantinople. Such negotiations for ecclesiastical independence would explain the papal embassies which visited Vladimir while he was in Kherson and shortly after his return to Kiev. Apparently the papal embassies could offer the newly formed Rus' church no more independence than Constantinople was willing to concede, and Vladimir and his church remained in the Byzantine jurisdiction.

Such is the chronology of the conversion of Russia. After the year 990 Rus' is officially reckoned a Christian nation. The facts which we have tried to chronicle and interpret have, however, more than an antiquarian interest. For the conversion was probably the most important single event in Russian history. Certainly the conversion to Christianity of each of the barbarian nations of Europe marked an important turning point in each nation's history. A Christianized tribe became different from a pagan tribe not only by dint of its Christianity *per se,* but also, and possibly more importantly, because the tribe automatically became, by its baptism, a part of Western Civilization. The baptized tribe took on a new and special relationship either to the Papacy in the West or to the Byzantine Empire in the East. The local culture received a new impetus and new forms from the new Christian orientation of the nation and, more practically, from the civilizing work of the missionaries, representatives of a higher and a Christian culture. In this respect the conversion of the Rus' was not essentially different from the conversion of any other tribe of Europe baptized by royal decree. What does distinguish the history of Christian Rus' from say, the history of Christian Poland or of Christian Sweden, is that Rus' was Christianized by Byzantium, by the Eastern rather than by the Western Church, and thereby eventually became an Orthodox rather than a Catholic country.

For many years it was fashionable to speak of the baneful influence of Byzantium on Russia. "Byzantine" came to mean sly, two-faced, decadent, and was used chiefly in the phrase "Byzantine intrigue," an expression conjuring up a picture of eunuchs plotting secretly in a vaulted chamber behind the throne of Constantinople. This was the sense in which people spoke of the "Byzantine influence" in Russia. The immensities of Ivan the Terrible were described as a typical expression of the Byzantine strain in the Russian soul. The unlimited autocracy of Imperial Russia and of its Communist successor state was explained as the modern fruit of the Byzantine culture once implanted in the Russian soul. Today, however, we are more likely to explain the darker aspects of Russian history by reference to the effects of Russia's long subjection to a truly oriental despotism, the Mongols.

In the same critical vein, the accusation often was raised that Russia cut itself off from Europe by joining the Byzantine church. The accusation is true, but only in a later period; the baptism of Rus' actually united the newly Christianized country to Christian Europe rather than separating Russia from Europe. While Russia's closest ties—cultural, commercial, and religious—were with the Byzantine Christian East in the Middle

Ages, her contacts with Western Europe were by no means restricted before the thirteenth century. Matrimonial ties between the ruling houses of Europe and Rus' were common, particularly those with central Europe and Scandinavia, constituent parts of the Western Church. Latin churches existed in several cities of Rus' to serve the needs of Western merchants, and, at least in the twelfth century, Rus' pilgrims were welcomed as brothers in the Latin Kingdom of Palestine. The separation of Russia from Western Europe came only in the thirteenth century. The behavior of the Latin Christian Crusaders towards the Greek Christians when the former captured Constantinople in 1204 broke the bond of unity between Christians in the East and West. Before the wound of separation could be healed, Russia was once more cut off from European Christianity by a nomadic iron curtain, the Mongol yoke. When the Mongol hold over Russia was finally broken, the Eastern and Western Churches had already developed so far in their own directions that neither was able to accept the other's line of evolution as being within the limits of traditional Christian development. Moreover, the Eastern and Western churches also found themselves in conflict over parts of Eastern Europe. Russia's struggle with Poland over the West Russian, Belorussian, and Ukrainian lands became a crusade of Orthodox East against Catholic West. This late medieval Russian distrust of the West was destined to outlive governmental commitment to the church affiliations which had become the battle cry for the first East-West conflicts.

Certain distinctly negative aspects of Byzantine influence in Russia must, however, be admitted. Important among these are a tendency towards religious ritualism at the expense of a fully expressed moral system, and the lack of a meaningful ideal for lay sanctity. These shortcomings hurt the Orthodox Church of Russia to the present day.

But the negative aspects of Byzantine influence in Russia have been given more than their due for many years. Less, however, has been said about the beneficial results of Vladimir's religious alliance with Byzantium. It should be rembered that the Byzantium to which Vladimir turned for Christianity and culture in 988 was at the peak of its medieval power and glory. In the tenth century Constantinople was not only the cultural capital of the Christian world, but, for all its periodic revolts, it was also the political center of a large and strong empire. In short,

Vladimir could not have made a wiser choice of a mentor of civilization than Byzantium.

The wisdom of Vladimir's choice of Byzantium as a religious and cultural model is amply demonstrated by the rapid development of a Christian civilization in Kievan Rus'. Within a generation of Vladimir's conversion Kiev was described as a marvellous city with forty churches. The second generation of Christian princes of Rus' outdid the lavishness of even St. Vladimir in beautifying their cities with Christian monuments. Indeed, during the reign of Vladimir's son, Iaroslav the Wise, Kiev is described by a German visitor as second only to Constantinople in the wealth and beauty of its churches and in the level of its cultural life. The magnificent Kievan churches of St. Sophia and of the Caves Monastery stood as eminent examples of the heights to which East Christian architecture, mosaic decoration, and painting reached in the period, while the large churches of the provincial cities of Rus' pointed towards the Russian ecclesiastical art destined to develop on Byzantine foundations in succeeding generations.

Christianity is not, however, a matter of church buildings, but a special world view. This too immediately took hold in the centers of Rus' and bore literary fruits in a matter of one or two generations. In explaining the unprecedented development of a Christian culture in Rus' within a generation or two of the "baptism of the Rus'," one must look to a custom peculiar to the Eastern Church in the Middle Ages the use of the vernacular as a liturgical and literary language. More specifically, much of the literary and liturgical heritage of Byzantium was immediately available to the young Church of Rus' in its own tongue. The Bulgarian church had been a Slavic-speaking part of the Eastern Church for a hundred years before Vladimir's conversion, and had amassed a wealth of Slavic translations of Byzantine materials, mostly religious, through zeal for things Byzantine in high Bulgarian circles. The newly founded Rus' church could, as it were, "plug into" Bulgaro-Byzantine culture and soon be one hundred years ahead culturally.

The young Rus' church did indeed build on a Bulgaro-Byzantine foundation. The flowering of literature in eleventh-century Kievan Rus' bespeaks not only talented writers, but also sophisticated readers. Sermons, chronicles, saints' lives, all show a highly refined literary taste, nurtured on Slavic translations of Byzantine originals. Yet the literary and intellectual culture of eleventh-century Rus' is not merely the result of the availability of fine models in an intelligible language. Rus' proved to be more than a passive receiver of Byzantine culture. Vladimir ordered all upper-class children to attend the schools which he had founded, where they were to learn reading, writing, and Christianity. The students became the teachers, writers, and preachers of the succeeding generation. Greek artists and singers trained the newly-converted Rus' in ecclesiastical painting and chant, which they, in turn, developed according to their own tastes and spread all over Rus'. Grand Prince Iaroslav, himself a diligent reader, supported secular and church schools, founded and endowed libraries in many Rus' cities and maintained a large body of translators to provide Rus' with even more Slavic translations of Byzantine religious materials, while at the same time supporting the production of original literary works. The results of these efforts are the highly civilized and profoundly Christian writings of Kievan Rus'.

The immediate availability of a wealth of Christian literature in the vernacular had one obvious disadvantage for Rus'; it made a serious study of classical languages unnecessary. The result is that Rus' had access to the writings of the Church fathers and to the classical heritage of Greece and Rome only through what happened to have been translated into Slavic. Translation was often accidental. It is easy to forget that an eloquent preacher of Kievan Rus' did not have access to a complete Bible, or access to more than fragmentary excerpts from the great treasury of writings of the Church Fathers. Thus it was that serious theological and philosophical thought was absent in Medieval Rus'.

A renaissance was not to be expected in a country where Latin and Greek, the necessary keys to classical thought, were all but unknown, and Russia never did have a renaissance. But neither did Russia experience a reformation, or even serious anti-clericalism. Russian clergymen were not raised above, and hence separated from, the laity by their knowledge of an arcane tongue. A literate layman had at his disposal all that a cleric did. Indeed, in Kievan Rus', as in Byzantium, it was the government, as much as the church, which fostered education. Literacy among urban laymen in early Rus' seems to have been but slightly behind lay literacy in Byzantium. When a daughter of Prince Iaroslav of Kiev married King Henry I of France in 1061, she, a woman could sign her name in Slavic and Latin, the language of her adopted homeland, while her royal husband scrawled his "X."

Yet another effect of the adoption of vernacular Christianity in Rus' may be suggested: direct exposure of the new Christians to the Gospel message. The simplicity of the Slavic translations of the Gospels made their message immediately intelligible to peasant, prince, and scholar alike, without the medium of priest or sermon. As one might expect in such circumstances, the simple precepts of the Gospels impressed the people far more than the complex rules of the Church. The simple, uncomplicated teachings of Christ were accepted at face value by the new Christians in Rus'. Prince Vladimir, for example, doubtless forgiving "forty times forty," did not to punish brigands in the first years after his baptism. His duty in this regard was quickly pointed out by the more sophisticated Greek clergy. The first martyrs of the Rus' church were two of Vladimir's sons, Boris and Gleb. They refused to raise their hands against their murderers (henchmen of their own brother), and died rather than injure another. Popular acclaim canonized Boris and Gleb for their Christ-like deaths long before the Greek hierarchy would allow the cult of such strange martyrs. A tradition of such Christ-like "non-resistance to evil" stretches from Boris and Gleb through the Russian sectarians of the seventeenth century to Lev Tolstoi and perhaps beyond. Similarly long is the vital Russian popular tradition of seeing Christ in all unfortunates (I was hungry and you gave me to eat; I was naked and you clothed me). As late as the early part of this century people in Russia would run after prisoners on their way to Siberia to press a coin into the hand of "the unfortunate Christ."

The social duties of a Christian became, as a matter of fact, the means to salvation for the layman in medieval Rus'. St. Vladimir became a hero of Russian folklore not only because of his Christianization of the country, but also because of his extreme generosity and hospitality. Vladimir is remembered for his banquets to which he invited not only the nobles and officers of his realm, but also the poor, the sick, and the infirm of Kiev. Those too ill to come to the palace were served from wagon loads of food brought to the poor neighborhoods. How deeply the concept of Christian duty penetrated the hearts of Rus' rulers is shown by the "Testament" of

Vladimir Monomakh, a twelfth century ruler of Kiev. In his final exhortation to his sons, Monomakh stresses a ruler's duty "to give to the orphan, to protect the widow, and to permit the mighty to destroy no man."

The growth of monasteries also betokened a quickening Christian life in the country. Monasteries in Rus', as is often the case, served the nation as centers of charity, hospitals, old age homes, and hospices for the increasing number of pilgrims on their way to pray at Christian shrines. The monasteries produced saints very quickly, great ascetics saving their souls by rigid discipline in seclusion and simple folk saving their souls by the love of God made fruitful in community life. The monks most respected for their sanctity served as confessors to the laity, and often as consciences to the ruling princes, ameliorating their feuds and tempering their justice.

By the time of the Mongol conquest of Rus' in 1240, urban Rus' was Christian and possessed a vital religious life, boasting fifteen dioceses and at least seventy monasteries and convents. The impact of Christianity on rural Russia was, however, still far from complete. Many of the scattered villages in the countryside had adopted what was, at most, a thin veneer of Christian practices over a base of strong folk paganism. The conversion of the great masses of the peasantry came only after the Mongol conquest had utterly destroyed the chief cities of Rus'.

The devastation and dislocation caused by the great Mongol sweep across Rus' affected the Church as it did all other institutions. When the church began to rebuild itself in the devastated land, it could only, because of the destruction of the cities, address itself to the still largely unchristianized rural masses. The nature of the Byzantine church and the mode of its missionary work in Rus' made its mission much easier. Even more in the countryside than in the city the missionary value of the Byzantine liturgical services was evident. The simple peasant must have been immediately attracted by the ceremony and ritual of the Eastern Church, and by the rich magnificence of the churches in what was a dark and dreary time for the Russian subjects of the Mongol Empire. Once attracted to the building and to the ceremonies of the Church, the simple peasant was seduced by all he saw and heard and enjoyed. The icons and frescoes decorating the churches retold the stories of the Old and New

Testament, and presented in symbols the doctrine of the community of the church at worship with the church triumphant among the saints. The poetry of the Slavonic Byzantine liturgy which had enthralled the intelligentsia of urban Rus' brought to the beautiful story of Jesus, retold in the simple Slavonic words of the Gospel readings for each Sunday and holy day, an aura of mysticism, presenting the divinity with all its tremendous awesomeness. The simple Russian peasant met both Christ the merciful Saviour of the Gospels and God the fearful judge of the Old Testament— and found himself a Christian.

Monasteries began to be built in the countryside rather than in the cities, and the Rus' church began the program which had so regularly accompanied Christian missionary efforts in every land, the creative adopting of agrarian pagan rituals into the cycle of the Christian liturgical year. Old holidays of the agricultural Slavs were united to the feasts of the Christian year, and the whole cycle of yearly rural life became meaningful in the greater context of cosmic redemption through the life of Christ. As man was sanctified at birth by baptism, at marriage by the sacrament of matrimony, and at death by Christian burial, so was daily life consecrated by commemorations of the events which made up the life of Christ. This adaptation of local customs by the missionaries, sometimes an unwitting adoption of pagan practices, proved effective in converting the people of Rus'. The last pagan Slavic burial excavated by archeologists dates from the fourteenth century. From this period on, paganism seems no longer to be a real competitor with Christianity in the hearts of Russians.

The very strong position in which the Church found itself after the first wave of Mongol conquest simplified its task of preaching the Gospel. By 1266 the churches, monasteries, clergy high and low, and even peasants settled on ecclesiastical lands, had been exempted by the Mongols from all taxes and levies. The Church found itself, by dint of Mongol religious toleration, the strongest institution in Rus' economically and politically, and the only Rus' institution encouraged to grow by the land's non-Christian overlords. The wealth and power attained by the Church under the Mongol yoke allowed the Church to complete its mission of converting all Rus' to the Christian faith, and thereby to unite all Rus' around itself as a national center. The Church thus became so strong that soon after it had backed the first Russian assaults on the country's Mongol overlords in the fourteenth century, it came into conflict with the emerging Muscovite state. The balanced equilibrium between church and state characteristic of the East Christian world broke into a competition for men's loyalty. Eventually the state was to triumph. Russia's long awaited shaking off of Mongol rule put Russia on the threshold of the developing modern nation state, where the function of the Church was to become subsidiary to the purpose of government.

SUGGESTED READINGS

A number of the most interesting contemporary sources for the early history of Russian Christianity are available in English translation. Among these are *The Russian Primary Chronicle, Laurentian Text,* edited and translated by Samuel Hazzard Cross and Olgerd Sherbowitz-Wetzor (Cambridge, MA: Mediaeval Academy of America, 1953) and Georgii P. Fedotov, *A Treasury of Russian Spirituality* (New York: Harper & Row, 1965). A good statement of current scholarship on the facts surrounding the conversion of Rus' is A. Poppe, "The Political Background of the Baptism of Rus'," *Dumbarton Oaks Papers* 30 (1976), 195-244. On early Rus' spirituality see Georgii P. Fedotov, *The Russian Religious Mind,* 2 vols. (Cambridge, MA: Harvard University Press, 1946-66), which, however, overstates the differences between Byzantine and Rus' religious outlooks.

4

Arabic Perceptions of Russia's Christian Conversion

William E. Watson
University of Pennsylvania

Specialists in east European history have long recognized the significance of medieval Islamic geographical literature for the economic activities and customs of the early Rus' (ca. ninth-twelfth centuries A.D.). A number of nineteenth and twentieth-century east European and expatriate Arabists and Turkologists have examined most of the geographical sources and a voluminous secondary literature exists on them.[1] Scholars have not, however, made full use of the medieval historical literature composed in Arabic.[2] Arabic histories have mainly been used by Russian history specialists as a record of the activities of Rus' in the Caspian (B.A. Dorn and V.F. Minorsky).[3] It seems appropriate that in this millennial year of Christianity in Russia an examination should be made of the conversion of Kievan Rus' to Orthodox Christianity using the available Arabic historical evidence.[4]

Medieval Arabic and Farsì geographies contain a wealth of information concerning early commercial routes and trade goods of *ar-Rùs* (beginning with the first extant source, Ibn-Khurdàdhbih, ca. 850), as well as pre-Christian *Rùs* customs (for instance, Ibn-Rustah and Ibn Faḍlàn, in the early tenth century).[5] The Rus' city of Kiev is mentioned by Muslim authors beginning in the tenth century. The corpus of material found in al-Iṣtakhrì and Ibn Ḥawqal, as well as the *Hudud al-ʿAlam* and al-Idrìsì (among others) mention Kiev (*Kuyùbà*) and two other Rus' cities (*Ṣlà* perhaps referring to the *Slovene* of Novgorod, and the virtually unidentifiable *'Arthà*).[6] The earliest notices of the Rus' in Arabic and Farsì sources which relate to the Rurikids of Kiev are descriptions of the tenth-century Rus' piracy in the Caspian Sea region and the tenth- and eleventh-century Byzantine military operations in the Near East which included Rus'

mercenaries in the imperial armies.[7] Among the early references to the
Rurikids of Kiev in Arabic sources are accounts of the tenth-century
conversion of the Rus' to Constantinopolitan Orthodoxy.

Abù 'l-Faraj Yaḥya Ibn Saʿīd Ibn Yaḥya included the first of these into
his *Ta'rīkh*. Yaḥya Ibn Saʿīd († ca. 1066) was an Egyptian Melkite Christian who continued the Arabic historical examination of Saʿīd Ibn Batriq
(Eutychius) on the Orthodox Christian communities of Byzantium,
Egypt, and Syria.[8] According to the chronology of H. Gregoire and
M. Canard, Yaḥya emigrated to Byzantine Antioch in about 1014–15,
together with a great number of Christians and Jews who were being
persecuted by the eccentric Fāṭimid caliph, al-Ḥàkim (996–1021), who
imagined himself to be a deity (and whom the Druze still consider as
such).[9] Yaḥya completed the second version of his *Ta'rīkh* at Antioch,
using newly-found Greek and Syriac chronicles.[10] It is quite possible that
Yaḥya found the source(s) for his passage on the conversion of the Rus' in
Antioch.[11]

The decision of the Rus' prince Vladimir to convert to the faith of the
Byzantines in 988–89 was closely connected with several political events,
and, significantly, Yaḥya was aware of them. The details of his account are
corroborated by other sources for the conversion, such as *Russian Primary
Chronicle* and the *Chronographia* of Michael Psellus.[12] The hagiographical
material contained in the *Primary Chronicle* concerning Vladimir's vision
problem, however, as well as his examination of various faiths, is absent
from Yaḥya's account.[13] Nevertheless, his unnamed sources for the conversion were indeed well-informed, and his account is unquestionably
reliable

> This matter (the revolt of Bardas Phocas) became serious, and King Basil became
> worried about the strength of his troops, [feeling that] their exhaustion would
> [lead to] their defeat, and his resources were depleted. Out of necessity he sent
> for the king of the Rùs, although the Rus were his enemies, requesting assistance
> from them for the problem which was confronting him.

> The two of them contracted a marriage alliance. The Rùs king married the sister
> of Basil. Basil afterward imposed on the Rùs king the condition that he be
> baptised. The Rùs king went to the people of his country, and the Rùs are a great
> people. At that time the Rùs did not have a law nor did they have a religion, and
> so Basil sent metropolitans and bishops [to the Rùs]. Basil sent his sister to the
> Rùs king, and she built many churches in the land of the Rùs.

When the matter of the marriage was settled between Basil and the Rùs king, Rùs troops arrived and joined the soldiers of ar-Rùm who were with King Basil. All of the soldiers betook themselves by land and by sea to meet Bardas Phocas at Chrysopolis. They defeated Phocas, and Basil took possession of the coast, and he went to the ships which had been in the hands of Phocas.[14]

Unfortunately Yaḥya affixed no date to the conversion. The events in Bardas Phocas' revolt immediately preceding the summoning of Vladimir, however, are dated 14 *Aylùl* 1298/1 *jumada* 377, which is September 14, 987, according to the Gregorian calendar.[15]

Somewhat less informed than Yaḥya Ibn Saʿid is our next source for the Rus' conversion, Sharaf az-Zamàn Ṭàhir al-Marwàzì (*fl.* ca. 1120). Al-Marwàzì was a Muslim (perhaps a Shiite) born in the Central Asian city of Marv, but we know very little of his life. His *Ṭabàʾiʿ al-Ḥayawàn (The Nature of Animals)* is an Arabic work of geographical, anthropological, and zoological interest which was partially examined by A. J. Arberry and more fully by V. F. Minorsky.[16] The early part of his entry on the Rus', in which he briefly states that the Rus' lived on an island or peninsula (*jazira*) and that they were skillful swordsmen, is derived from a corpus of material used by Ibn Rustah, the anonymous author of the *Ḥudùd al ʿÀlam,* al-Muqaddasì, Gardìzì, and al-Bakrì.[17] The actual conversion account is somewhat puzzling:

This [earning of their livelihood by the sword] was the upbringing [of their young men] until they converted to Christianity in the year 300 [912 A.D.]. When they entered into Christianity, the faith blunted their swords and the door of their livelihood became closed to them. To them returned a disadvantaged state and poverty, and their livlihood diminished. Then they desired Islam, so that it would be lawful for them to conduct raids and holy war, and thus recover by a return to that which they had done before.

They sent four messengers who were relatives of their king to the ruler of Khwàrazm. Their king is called *Wladmir,* just as the king of the Turks is called *Khaqan* and the kings of the Bulghars is called *Ṭ-l-ṭù.* Their messengers came to Khwàrazm and delivered the message. The Khwàrazm-Shah was delighted by their desire for Islam, and he sent someone to teach them the religious laws of Islam.[18]

Al-Marwàzì subsequently relates several Rus' military ventures (Constantinople, Bardaʿa), implying that they were again a strong people as a result of their Islamic conversion.[19] Although Vladimir of Kiev did not commit an act of apostasy after his baptism, Minorsky suggested that the source of this material may have been a minor prince or nobleman called Vladimir (either as his personal name or a "generic designation") who may have expressed an interest in converting to Islam in Khwàrazm.[20] Minorsky added, however, that the story of the poverty experienced by the Rus' following their Christian conversion is clearly a variant form of the familiar Muslim criticism of Manichaeism and Christianity.[21]

Al-Marwàzì's passage on the double conversion of the Rus' is repeated by a prominent Persian Muslim author from Transoxania, Muḥammad Ibn Muḥammad Shadìd ad-Dìn ᶜAwfì, in his *Hikayàt* (*Anecdotes*), composed in Farsì before 1236.[22] ᶜAwfì also preserves the name of Vladimir, but he transcribes the Arabic preposition *bi* along with the Arabic transliteration of the name, and thus renders it as *Bùladmìr* (which in Farsì means "Prince of Steel").[23]

Much more in accordance with the Ta'rikh of Yaḥya Ibn Saᶜìd than al-Marwàzì and ᶜAwfì is the account of 'Izz ad-Dìn Abu l'Ḥasan Ibn al-Athìr, who was from an important Arab Muslim family of northern ᶜIràq. During the course of his scholarly career, most of which was spent in the city of Mosul, and which lasted until his death in 1233, he produced one of the greatest Arab historical works, *al-Kàmil fi 't-Ta'rikh* (*The Entirety of History*, hereafter referred to as *al-Kàmil*).[24]

Al-Kàmil is a history of the peoples of the *dàr al-Islàm*, as well as some of the peoples of the *dàr al-Ḥarb*, arranged in an annalistic fashion. Unfortunately, Ibn al-Athìr rarely cites his sources, and because many of them are probably no longer extant, we are unable to trace the origin and means of transmission of much of his material.[25] We know, however, that he borrowed much of his earlier material from aṭ-Ṭabarì († 923) and al-Balàdhurì († 892). We can also ascertain the sources of some of his notices of Rus' piracy in the Caspian Sea region and mercenary service in Byzantine Near Eastern campaigns (such as Ibn Miskawayh, al-Mutanabbì, and Abù Firàs, for instance).[26] We cannot, however, point to the origin of his conversion account.

Ibn al-Athìr placed the conversion of the Rus' between a notice on the career of a relatively minor political figure, Warad ar-Rùmì, and a passage on the Byzantine emperor Basil II Bulgaroctonos, which is remarkable for its very favorable assessment of the emperor. His account of the conversion reads as follows:

Waradis Ibn-Làwn went to Constantinople, and in it were the two kings who were the sons of 'Armanus, Basil and Constantine. Waradis harassed them, and they corresponded with the Rùs king, asking for his help and offering their sister to him in marriage. She refused, however, to hand herself over to one whose religion differed from her own.

Thus Rùs king then converted to Christianity and this was the beginning of Christianity among the Rùs. He married her, then he went to Waradis and they engaged in battle. Waradis was killed and the two kings established their dominion.[27]

Unlike Yaḥya Ibn Saʿìd, neither Ibn al-Aṯhìr nor al-Marwàzì indicate that they were familiar with Christian ecclesiastical titles. Yaḥya mentions the metropolitans *(maṭàrina)* and bishops *(ʾasàqifa)* who had been sent to the lands of the Rus' by Basil. Ibn al-Aṯhìr and al-Marwàzì mention neither these ecclesiastical figures nor the churches *(kanàʾis)* mentioned by Yaḥya. The Arabic verb used by both Ibn al-Aṯhìr and Al-Marwàzì to describe the conversion of Vladimir and the Rus' is *tanaṣṣara*, "to become a Christian." The use of the verb is quite predictable here. Yaḥya Ibn Saʿìd, on the other hand, uses to Arabic verb *ʿatamada*, "to be baptised," for Vladimir. In addition, he uses the Arabic verb *aʿmada* to describe what the bishops and metroplitans *did* to Vladimir and his people. It is, of course, not surprising that Yaḥya was more proficient in the ecclesiastical terminology of the Arabic language than was Ibn al-Aṯhìr or al-Marwàzì because he was a Christian and the latter two authors were Muslims.

Similarly, Yaḥya's placing of the conversion some time after the events of September 987 is more accurate than Ibn al-Aṯhìr's date for the conversion, which is 375 A.H. [985–86 A.D.] Ibn al-Aṯhìr's incorrect dating of this event is also not surprising, because few of his dates are precise, even for some of the contemporary events which he relates in *al-Kàmil*.[28] Nevertheless, Ibn al-Aṯhìr saw the Rus' as an important people of the *dàr al-Ḥarb*, worthy of inclusion in his universal history along with other important non-Muslim peoples such as the Byzantines *(ar-Rùmì)*. Al-Marwàzì's dating of the event as 312 A.H. [900 A.D.] is much less accurate. This is too early even for the conversion of Vladimir's grandmother Olga (ruled 945–62). The discrepancy in the dating of the event, as well as the inclusion of the unlikely story of the Islamic conversion of the Rus', makes his account less valuable that that of Yaḥya Ibn Saʿìd or Ibn al-Aṯhìr.

The historiographical significance of these accounts of the conversion of the Rus' to Christianity produced in the Near East and Central Asia lies not in the particular details on the conversion mentioned by the authors, but rather simply in their existence. It is highly significant that authors who had never visited Russia, and who had probably never met a Russian, wrote about the conversion. This interest on the part of the Arabic historians was the result of the ferocious reputation earned by the Rus' in Byzantine military expeditions in the Near East, as well as Rus' piracy in the Caspian Sea in the ninth, tenth, and eleventh centuries. The Arabic historical sources of the conversion of the Rus' are as worthy of scholarly attention as the more well-known European sources, such as the *Russian Primary Chronicle.*[29]

NOTES

1. From the many works produced by these scholars, see in particular A. E. Harkawi, *Skazaniia musul'manskikh pisatelei o slavanakh i russkikh* (1870, The Hague, 1969, Mouton) I. I. Krachkovskii, *Istoriia arabskoi geograficheskoi literatury* (Moscow, 1957) V. V. Bathold, 'Novoe musul'manskoe isvestie o russakh,' in his *Sochineniia*_ii, 1 (Moscow, 1963) V. F. Minorsky, *Ḥudud al ʿÀlam The Regions of the World, a Persian Geography* (Karachi, 1980) D. A. Khvol'son, *Izvestiia o Khazarakh, Butasakh, Bolgarakh, Madjarakh, Slavanakh i Russakh Abu-Ali Achmeda Ben Omar Ibn-Dasta (Ibn Rustah).* (St. Petersburg, 1869) T. Lewicki, *Zródla arabskie do dziejów Sowianszczyzny* (Warsaw, 1956-69) B. N. Zakhoder, *Kaspiiskii svod svedenii o vostochnoi Evrope* (Moscow, 1962-67) I Hrbek, "Der dritte Stamm der Rüs nach arabischen Quellen," *Archiv Orientali* 25 (1957), pp. 628-52 O. Pritsak, "An Arabic text on the Trade Route of the Corporation of Ar-Rus in the Second Half of the Ninth Century," *Folia Orientalia* 12 (1970), 241-59.

2. The problems involved are discussed by G. Makdisi, "Western Orientalism and Muslim Religious History," in M. L. Swartz, Ed., *Studies on Islam* (New York, 1981), pp. 217-28.

3. B. A. Dorn, "Caspia, Über die Einfälle der alten Russen in Tabaristan," in *Mémoires de l'academie impériale des sciences de Saint-Pétersbourg,* ser. 7, t. 23, n. 1 (St. Petersburg, 1877) V. F. Minorsky, *A History of Sharvan and Darband* (Cambridge, U.K., 1958).

4. An early cursory discussion of the sources for the conversion was made by Minorsky in his article "Rus," *Encyclopaedia of Islam* (first edition) p. 1182.

5. Ibn Khurdàdhbih, *Kitàb al-Masàlik wa 'l-Mamàlik,* ed. by M. J. De Goeje. Bibliotheca Arabicorum Geographorum [BGA] (Leiden, 1889), 154 Ibn

Rustah, *Kitàb al-Aᶜlàk an-Nafìsa,* ed. by M. J. de Goeje, BGA (Leiden, 1892), vii, 145-47 Z. V. Togan, "Ibn Fadlan's Reisebericht," in *Abhandlungen für die Kunde des Mörgenlandes* (Leipzig, 1939), xxiv3. An important collection of the Arabic souces for this area was compiled in Oslo by Alexander Seippel entitled *Rerum Normannicarum Fontes Arabici* (1876-1928).

6. Al-Iṣṭakhrì, *Kitàb al-Masàlik wa 'l-Mamàlik,* ed. M. al-Hinì (Cairo, 1961), p. 132 Ibn Ḥawqal, *Kitàb Ṣurat al-Arḍ,* trans. by J. H. Kramers, G. Wiet, *Configuration de la terre* (Paris, 1964) v. 2, pp. 387-88 V. F. Minorsky, trans. *Ḥudùd al ᶜAlam,* p. 159 al-Idrisi, *Kitàb Nazha al-Mashtaq fì Akhtiràk al-Afàq,* ed. I. Seippel, *Rerum Normannicarum,* p. 86. See I. Hrbek, *Op. Cit.,* O. Pritsak, "The Name of the Third Kind of Rus and of Their City," *Journal of the Royal Asiatic Society,* pt. 1 (1967), pp. 2–9 P. B. Golden, "The Question of the Rus' Qaganate," *Archivum Eurasiae Medii Aevi* 2 (1982), *passim.*

7. Among the many authors who recorded the activities of the Rus' in the Caspian (extending into the Caucasus) were al-Masᶜùdì, *Murùj adh-Dhahab wa Maᶜàdìn al-Jawàhìr,* ed. and trans. by C. B. de Meynard and P. De Courteille, *Les Prairies d'or* (Paris, 1863), v. 2, pp. 18–25 Ibn Miskawayh, *Tajarub al-Umam,* ed. by H. F. Amedroz (Baghdad, n.d.), v. 2, pp. 62-63 Ibn al-Athir, *al-Kamil fì 't-Ta'rikh,* ed. Dar Sader and Dar Beyrouth (Beirut, 1965), v. 8, pp. 412-15. See V. F. Minorsky, *Sharvan and Darband* B. A. Dorn, "Caspia," *passim.* Among those who mentioned Rus' service in Byzantine military operations are Ibn al-Athìr, *al-Kàmil,* v. 8, p. 508 v. 10, p. 65 Ibn Ẓàfir, *Kitàb ad-Duwul al-Munqatìᶜa,* trans. by M. Canard in A. A. Vasiliev, *Byzance et les arabes* (Brussels, 1950), v. 2, p. 125 Ibn al-Qalànisi, *Ta'rìkh Dimashq,* ed. by H. F. Amedroz (Leiden, 1908), p. 43.

8. H. Gregoire and M. Canard in A. A. Vasiliev, *Byzance et les arabes* (Brussels, 1950), v. 2, p. 80.

9. *Ibid,* pp. 81–82.

10. Among the sources which Yaḥya used were the common, unnamed Byzantine Greek sources of the Continuator of Theophanes, Symeon Magister, and Leo the Grammarian. See Vasiliev, *Byzance et les arabes,* p. 86.

11. As his description of the Rus' conversion is much more in accordance with the European sources (Byzantine, Russian) than with the other Arabic sources, we must assume that the source of his material was Byzantine Greek in origin.

12. *The Russian Primary Chronicle Laurentian Text,* trans. and ed. by S. H. Cross and O. P. Sherbowitz-Wetzor (Cambridge, Mass., 1953), pp. 110-117 Michael Psellus, *Chronographia,* ed. and trans. by E. R. A. Sewter, *Fourteen Byzantine Rulers* (Hammondsworth, Middlesex, U. K., 1966), pp. 34-35. D. Obolensky considers the account to be highly accurate. See his *The Byzantine Common-wealth* (London, 1971), pp. 255, 259.

13. *The Russian Primary Chronicle,* ed. Cross and Sherbowitz-Wetzor, pp. 110–17.

14. Yaḥya Ibn Saᶜìd, *Ta'rìkh,* ed. and trans. by I. I. Krachkovskii and A. A. Vasiliev

in *Patrologia Orientalis* (Paris, 1932) t. 23, fasc. 2, pp. 423-24.

15. *Ibid,* p. 423.

16. V. F. Minorsky, *Sharaf al-Zamàn Ṭàhir Marvazì on China, the Turks and India* (London, 1942), pp. 1-2.

17. *Ibid.,* p. 118. For this material, see also the comments of P. B. Golden, "The Question of the Rus' Qaganate," pp. 82, 89, 92.

18. *Ibid.,* p. *23. I have consulted Minorsky's translation on page 36.

19. *Ibid.* These campaigns were, of course, mentioned by other Arabic authors (see above, note 8). None of these authors, however, wrote of the supposed Islamic conversion of the Rus' described by al-Marwàzì.

20. *Ibid.,* p. 119. O. Pritsak has taken this passage quite literally a believes that it actually refers to St. Vladimir of Kiev! See his *The Origin of Rus'* (Cambridge, Mass., 1981), v. 1, xvi.

21. *Ibid.*

22. For biographical information on ʿAwfi, see M. Nizàmuddin, " ʿAwfi," *Encyclopaedia of Islam,* second edition, p. 764.

23. Minorsky, *Marvazì,* p. 118, n. 3.

24. See the discussion of F. Rosenthal, "Ibn al-Athìr," *Encyclopaedia of Islam,* second edition, pp. 723-25.

25. For brief discussions of *isnad* as employed by medieval Arabic historians, see H. A. R. Gibb, *'Tarikh,'* reprinted in *Studies on the Civilization of Islam* (Princeton, 1982), pp. 111, 120 N. Faruqi, *Early Muslim Historiography* (Delhi, 1979), p. 196.

26. Ibn Miskawayh, *Tajarub al-Umam,* v. 2, pp. 62-63 al Mutanabbi in A. A. Vasiliev, *Byzance et les arabes,* v. 2, p. 331 Abu Firas in *Ibid.,* v. 2, p. 364.

27. Ibn al-Athìr, *al-Kàmil fì 't-Ta'rìkh,* v. 9, pp. 43–44.

28. For example, his misdating of some events in the crusades is mentioned by F. Gabrieli, *Arab Historians of the Crusades* (Berkeley, 1984), *passim.*

29. This paper was read at the University of Oregon's symposium on "The Millennium Christianity and Russia (A.D. 988-1988)," April 11, 1988. I wish to thank Dr. Albert Leong, Dr. Alan Kimball, and Dr. A. Dean McKenzie of the University of Oregon for kindly inviting me to participate in the conference. I also wish to thank Dr. Alexander V. Riasanovsky of the University of Pennsylvania for reading an earlier version of this paper, and offering his suggestions.

5

The Ukrainian Church: Observations on the Occasion of its Millennium

Basil Dmytryshyn
Portland State University

To be living at the appropriate time to participate in commemorating an important event of 1,000 years ago is rare good fortune and a unique privilege. In this instance the event was the acceptance of Christianity as the official faith of his realm by Prince Vladimir, ruler of Kievan Rus'. It is gratifying to know that this epoch-making event is being observed throughout the world in 1988. A review of the events scheduled worldwide suggests that this commemoration will produce many meetings, speeches, articles, and books by scholars as well as by religious people. Since they will approach the topic from their unique perspectives there will be neither consensus nor uniformity in their views. This is the way it should be, because such a vital happening as the acceptance of Christianity cannot be reduced to a single interpretation or formula. To do so would be a disservice as well as a distortion.

This being the case, I would like to suggest that a Ukrainian view or perception of the acceptance of Christianity and of the subsequent trials and tribulations of the Church there can be appreciated and fully understood only if we are aware of the complex historic practice, spirit, and experience of other East European, Slavic, Orthodox nations. This practice and experience reveal that there are several closely intertwined and deeply ingrained beliefs. Foremost is the feeling that religious and national affiliations are inseparable. In fact, East and South Slav nations always identified their national existence with their church. This religious-national identity, in turn, has been responsible for the religious division among the Slavs. So profound, indeed, has been this division that it has prevented the emergence of a supreme religious Orthodox authority (cf. the Pope) to guide and coordinate the activity of various national units. As a result, each national church that has existed has been governed by a council of bishops (pro-forma presided over by a metropolitan or a patriarch) all of whom, however, actually were selected and controlled by secular leaders. In short, the *modus fidei* as well as the *modus operandi* in every Orthodox entity in Eastern Europe has been guided by the principle of *cuius regio eius religio,* that is, those who exercised the political power over a given region also had the right to determine the dogma, the structure, and the personnel of the church.

How do these complex beliefs and practices apply to Ukraine? It should be emphasized for the record that 1,000 years ago, when Christianity was introduced to that part of Eastern Europe, there was no Ukraine as this term is understood today. Similarly, there was no Russia at that time. These terms, Ukraine and Russia, came into use only in the seventeenth and the eighteenth centuries. When Christianity came to the region 1,000 years ago there was an entity called *Kievan Rus'.* That entity, whose frontiers were vaguely defined, included the basins of the Dnepr and the Volkhov rivers; the upper reaches of the Volga basin; the basin of the Dniester River and a few other areas. These territories were then inhabited by such Eastern Slavic tribes as Slavs, Krivichians, Dregovichians, Dulebians, Radimichians, Severians, Polianians, Volynians, Buzhians, Viatichians, and others. Although they maintained some contacts with each other, each tribe led its own semi-independent existence.

Kievan Rus' was not a unified or a centralized state, even though from the late ninth century it was ruled by members of the Rurik dynasty. Kievan Rus' was an association of semi-independent principalities whose ruling princes cooperated on some issues (as relatives often do) and disagreed most of the time on other issues (as relatives also frequently do). Indeed, the history of Kievan Rus' (from 880 until its demise in 1240) abounds more in conflicts than in cooperation among the many ambitious members of the Rurik dynasty. To view the history of Kievan Rus' in any other way is to take a great liberty with known historical facts. Twisting history to suit modern concepts or views amounts to retroactive distortion.

Christian ideas and practices came to the southern regions of Kievan Rus', i.e., present-day Ukraine, from such diverse sources as: (1) Jewish and Greek settlements in the Crimea; (2) Christian Goths after they were converted to the Arian "heresy"; (3) Roman legionnaires stationed in Dacia (present-day Romania); (4) efforts of the followers of Sts. Cyril and Methodius, who preached in the Moravian kingdom and doubtless in present-day Eastern Slovakia, the Lemko region of Poland, and the Zakarpatska *oblast* (district) of the Ukrainian Soviet Socialist Republic; (5) Varangian Christian converts (merchants and warriors) who traveled through Kievan Rus' on their way to Constantinople; and (6) Christian missionaries who were active in Kiev and Tmutorokan (present-day Kerch peninsula). After establishing itself formally in Kiev in 988, Christianity advanced slowly northward to Smolensk, Novgorod, Suzdal', Riazan', and some 160 years later, to Moscow.

There were many reasons why the southern regions of Kievan Rus were the first recipients of the benefits of Christianity. Long before Christianity became the official faith of its people, Kiev was the principal center of economic, cultural, and political activity. In that capacity Kiev served as *primus inter parem* for other towns and principalities and it also attracted adventurers, travellers, merchants, and missionaries of various persuasions. Moreover, Kiev was relatively close to Constantinople, the capital of the Byzantine empire, with which it maintained close economic and, later, cultural and dynastic ties.

Because Kiev and its southern environs possessed extraordinary vitality, many present-day Ukrainians believe that their forefathers were the principal beneficiaries of Byzantine civilization. Obviously, this claim is an exaggeration. But even if it is only partially true it is still important, for, with the possible exception of Baghdad, Constantinople was in the tenth century the most brilliant cultural, political, and economic center of the world as Kiev and the Western world knew it. Directly and indirectly through its economic, dynastic, and cultural links with Constantinople, Kievan Rus' was transformed into a civilized country. Christianity played the most significant role in this transformation because Christianity meant civilization.

Through Christianity, the people of Kievan Rus' acquired from the Byzantines the skill of building stone churches and the art of decorating them with icons, mosaics, and inscriptions. From Constantinople they also adopted the Church Slavonic alphabet and language, ecclesiastical terminology, phraseology, syntax, religious dogma, rituals, service books, prayers, chants, the Old and the New Testaments, teachings of many Church Fathers, Byzantine codes and chronicles, and many other works. Under the influence of these Byzantine examples, the ancestors of modern Ukrainians soon produced their own masterpieces. Space will not allow the listing of Byzantine works that influenced Kiev and the Kievan works that were influenced by Byzantine examples. One thing is clear, however. Regardless of whether it was translated or transplanted, secular or religious, artistic or architectural, Byzantine or Kievan, these achievements of the eleventh and the twelfth centuries compare very favorably with those produced at that time in Western Europe.

The only thing that Kievan Rus failed to achieve during this period was *political unity and independence on a prolonged and sustained basis* which could form an essential prerequisite for religious independence. Kievan Rus', as noted earlier, continued to exist as an assortment of semi-independent principalities. It had no single spokesman to defend its vital interests. In religious matters Kievan Rus' was a Metropolitanate and, as such, it was under the jurisdiction of the Patriarch of Constantinople. Most of the metropolitans were either Greek or Bulgarian ecclesiastics who defended Byzantine, not Kievan, interests. This, of course, was both proper and natural under the existing Byzantine practice and tradition.

The failure of Kievan Rus' to establish viable political unity on a prolonged and sustained basis produced other negative results. The first was a period of protracted, bloody civil war among the ambitious members of the Rurik dynasty that pitted brothers, cousins, nephews, uncles, and other relatives against one another. The struggle was devastating, resulting in murder, destruction of property, disruption of the economy, and the suffering of many innocent people. So bitter and so ruinous at times was this princely conflict that many contemporary records attributed it to the wrath of God. This attribution was made not because the opinions were written by churchmen, but because even the church a unifying institution of the country was powerless to prevent or to stop it.

The absence of political unity of Kievan Rus' also was responsible for the devastating raids on the country by such nomads as the Pechenegs, the Polovtsians, the Torks, and others. Some of these nomads were attracted to Kievan Rus' by its economic prosperity as well as by the political vacuum caused by incessant dynastic struggles. Others were invited by feuding members of the Rurik dynasty. Regardless of what instigated them, these annual raids inflicted enormous material destruction and heavy human casualties, since the nomads killed those who resisted, took others into captivity, and forced the rest to flee for safety to the northeast (Vladimir and Suzdal'), to the north (Smolensk, Pskov, and Novgorod), and to the west (Galicia and Volyn). These internal convulsions reduced Kievan Rus', once a prosperous and flourishing entity of semi-independent principalities, to a wasteland.

In the thirteenth century the political, economic, and cultural fortunes of Kievan Rus' were further profoundly affected by several external developments. The first two were closely related and came in the early part of the century. One involved the sacking of Constantinople in 1204 by the Fourth Crusade. The other, a direct aftermath of the first, was the shift of the spiritual, cultural, and economic activity from Byzantium to Italy. Two other blows came in the middle of the century. One was the rise of the mighty Mongol Empire, whose western unit (known in historical literature as the Golden Horde or the Kipchak Khanate) gained full control in 1240 of the entire southern section of Kievan Rus'. The other, which happened at about the same time, was the sudden emergence of the powerful state of Lithuania whose ambitious leaders incorporated numerous territories of Kievan Rus' into their domains.

These developments, caused by both internal and external forces, had a profound impact on Kievan Rus' and its people. They halted the fratricidal struggle, but they also destroyed Kiev's economy and terminated the country's political existence. They resulted, of course, in heavy casualties and forced many survivors to seek safety elsewhere. Among the refugees was the Metropolitan of Kiev who re-established his official residence in Vladimir where it remained until his successors transferred it to Moscow. Those few survivors who stayed in Kiev and its environs were compelled to acknowledge foreign domination and to accept a new allegiance.

Then between 1380 and 1450 four additional factors entered the arena and imposed new complexities. The first was the sudden rise, as a major power in Eastern Europe, of an obscure principality called

Muscovy. Its rulers attracted a number of followers who helped them to challenge the Mongol domination successfully and assume the position of sole legitimate successors to the entire heritage of Kievan Rus' and rightful protectors of all Eastern Slavic Orthodox Christians. The second event was an equally sudden rise of a powerful Catholic Polish-Lithuanian Commonwealth whose territories included also the basins of the Dnepr and the Dniester Rivers the two former core regions of Kievan Rus', inhabited by the ancestors of present-day Belorussians and Ukrainians. The third development was gradual disintegration of the once mighty Kipchak Khanate into several warring units. And the fourth was the emergence of a powerful Ottoman Empire, whose armies conquered the entire Balkan peninsula and in 1453 captured Constantinople, thus terminating the existence of the Byzantine Empire. Soon, however, a fierce conflict developed among the three empires (Polish-Lithuanian, Muscovite, and Ottoman) for control of the rich and strategically vital Ukraine. This struggle went on until the end of the eighteenth century, when Russian armies dismembered the Polish-Lithuanian Commonwealth, inflicted a near mortal blow to the Ottoman Empire, and gained full control of the Ukraine.

These developments exerted a momentous political, intellectual, and psychological impact on the ancestors of present-day Ukrainians. Centuries-old foreign domination and the prolonged struggle among the three empires over Ukrainian territories prevented the establishment of an independent Ukrainian state, a *conditio sine qua non* to the existence of an independent church and its hierarchy. The Ukrainians were instead subordinated to such foreign centers as Warsaw and Moscow, where they were distrusted for harboring ambitions of political and religious independence and where they were reduced to the status of second class Christians.

During this prolonged period of foreign domination each power tried to de-nationalize as well as re-Christianize the Ukrainians. The Russians forcibly imposed Russian Orthodoxy on Ukrainians under their control, while the Poles pressured those they controlled to embrace Roman Catholicism. Each power, too, dealt firmly with those Ukrainians who either refused to cooperate with official policies or who failed to appreciate their wisdom. Uncooperative Ukrainians were branded as recalcitrant nationalists, had their properties confiscated, their freedoms curtailed, and their opportunities for advancement eliminated. To escape these labels, discrimination, and persecution, some Ukrainians joined their masters. Many, however, remained silent. Some fought back, and some opted for Western affiliations.

The last point—Western affiliations—is significant because many present-day Ukrainians believe that their ancestors, unlike other East European Orthodox Slavs, sought throughout their history to establish close links with Western Europe. In support of this position they cite the following evidence from the Kievan Rus' period of history: (1) the attempt by Princess Ol'ga in 959-61 to establish a religious link with the church hierarchy of the Holy Roman Empire; (2) the effort by Prince Iziaslav of Kiev in 1073 to enlist support of Pope Gregory VII in an attempt to regain his Kiev principality; (3) visits to Kiev by a number of West European missionaries on their way to convert nomads encamped along the Volga; (4) countless intermarriages between Kievan princes and princesses and their West European counterparts; (5) the veneration in Kievan Rus' of several West European (i.e., Catholic) saints, some of whom were not recognized by either the Byzantine or Russian Orthodox Churches; (6) the military involvement of Prince Roman of Galicia-Volyn in a dynastic conflict in the Holy Roman Empire in 1205; (7) the attendance of Metropolitan Peter of Kiev at the ecumenical council that met in Lyons, France, in 1245 to work out a common Christian policy vis-a-vis the Mongols; and (8) the Papal offering of a royal crown to Prince Daniel of Galicia in 1247.

Notwithstanding these and many other efforts, the ancestors of present-day Ukrainians failed to establish a close, working link with Western Europe on a sustained and prolonged basis. This failure stemmed from the fact that until 1204 Constantinople wielded enormous power and attraction; that the Patriarch of Constantinople was opposed to every contact with "Latin heretics"; that (after 1240) the leadership of the Golden Horde vetoed every sign of such relations; that (after 1450) leaders of Moscow were set against it; and that the Ukrainians did not have their own independent state on a permanent basis that would enable them to chart their own destiny.

The only, albeit partially, successful expression of a prolonged Ukrainian linkage with Western Europe came at the end of the sixteenth century with the birth of the Uniate (currently known as the Greek Catholic) Church in the Polish-Lithuanian Commonwealth. Of the many complex factors making possible the appearance of this church (by formal decisions at Brest Litovsk in 1596 and in Uzhgorod in 1646), the following seem to have played the most critical role: (1) interference into religious and other matters of that part of the Polish-Lithuanian Commonwealth that was inhabited by Orthodox Christians by the Patriarch of Constantinople who, after 1453, was under Ottoman Turkish control; (2) interference into Polish-Lithuanian affairs by the political and religious leadership of Moscow; (3) interference into the activities of local Orthodox bishops by the self-appointed spokesmen of the *bratstva*, i.e., brotherhoods, who based their actions on vaguely defined instructions of the Patriarch of Constantinople; (4) hope entertained by some reform-minded bishops that in the aftermath of the Reformation the Pope would be in a good position to introduce needed church reforms in the Polish-Lithuanian Commonwealth; (5) hope harbored by some Jesuits who, after seeing parts of Western Europe going over to the Protestant cause, sought to gain a bridgehead to the Orthodox East, including Muscovy; and (6) support of the Uniate movement by Polish King Sigismund III, an enemy of the Turks, the Muscovites, the Protestants, and the political independence-minded Ukrainians.

The Uniate Church gained strength gradually and has survived to the present day because it allowed the use of Church-Slavonic language in the liturgy; because it approved the prevailing practice of married priesthood; because it left untouched the presence of icons and the iconostasis in the church; because it allowed the use of leavened bread in communion; and because, except for substituting Pope for Patriarch, it allowed the liturgy to remain essentially the same. In short, the Uniate Church survived because it neither introduced any drastic changes in the prevailing practices nor imposed any radical views or demands on its followers. This is not to suggest that the Uniate Church had the support of the majority of the Ukrainian population. Like all movements it initially attracted a few idealists and opportunists who hoped, by switching their religious affiliation, to gain personal advantage. In this regard the Uniates were not an exception but a general rule, since all movements throughout recorded history have attracted both idealists and opportunists. The majority of the population either remained indifferent or stuck with the old. This created a deep cleavage which, in spite of efforts to narrow it, persists to the present day.

From its inception to the present, the Uniate Church has encountered hostility from religious and political leaders in Moscow. The main reason for this has been the fact that the Uniate Church has its spiritual center in Rome, hence outside Moscow's jurisdiction and control. Until the reign of Catherine II the opposition was verbal. Following her dismemberment of the Polish-Lithuanian Commonwealth at the end of the eighteenth century that brought many Uniates under Russian control, Russian treatment of the Uniates assumed new dimensions. In 1795 Catherine abolished several Uniate dioceses, forced many to embrace either Russian Orthodoxy or Roman Catholicism, dispatching to Siberia those who resisted her order, and closed down several monasteries belonging to the Basilian Order, confiscating their property. It is interesting to note that the Empress left properties of the Jesuit Order undisturbed.

During the reigns of Paul I and Aleksandr I the anti-Uniate drive in the Russian Empire subsided, but it resumed under Nicholas I, who closed down additional monasteries belonging to the Basilian Order and arrested many Uniate priests for alleged participation in the 1830-31 Polish insurrection. In 1835 he subordinated the Uniate Church to the Office of the Ober-Procurator of the Holy Synod; and in February, 1839, he formally dissolved the Uniate-Catholic agreement of 1596 and sent many Uniate priests to Siberia or to Russia's interior. His son and successor, Aleksandr II, persecuted Uniates in the Kholm and Pidliasie regions (in the 1870's); and, during their brief stay in Galicia during World War I, Russian authorities arrested and deported many Uniates, including Metropolitan Andrew Sheptyckii, to Russia's interior.

The Uniates suffered terribly under Soviet dictator Joseph V. Stalin after he incorporated Galicia, Volyn, Bukovina, and Carpatho-Ukraine into the USSR. In all of those areas Soviet authorities arrested all Uniate bishops and many priests, tried them for alleged cooperation with the Nazis, and sentenced them to long prison terms. Of those arrested at that time one survived: Metropolitan Iosif Slipyi. He was released in 1963, thanks to personal intervention on his behalf by Pope John XXIII. In

March, 1946, Soviet authorities formally dissolved the Uniate Church, prohibited all Uniate activity, confiscated all Uniate property, and turned over those Uniate churches that had not been destroyed to officials of the Russian Orthodox Church. These measures remained firmly in place until the mid-1980s when the Soviets terminated their jamming of the Voice of the Vatican that broadcasts Sunday Mass in Ukrainian to the USSR. All indications are that Soviet officials, as well as many educated Russians, today view the Uniates as the lowest among Christians.

It should be noted that, although some Poles supported the movement, the Uniates as a group encountered many obstacles, abuses, and discriminations under Polish rule. This was because the Ukrainians had no political leverage within the Polish-Lithuanian Commonwealth, because the Uniate church was not a mass movement, because for many years Catholic Poles considered Uniates inferior to Roman Catholics, and because Roman Catholic Polish nobles enjoyed extensive political, economic, and social rights and privileges, while Ukrainian Uniates were predominantly serfs burdened with many obligations and deprived of all rights and opportunities. To escape these liabilities some Uniate nobles and even high clergy joined Roman Catholicism, while the masses periodically sought to establish a dialogue with their Ukrainian Orthodox brethren. Their efforts produced no satisfactory results because of the opposition of the Ukrainian cossacks, the influential Ukrainian Orthodox nobles and ecclesiastics, and Russian political and religious leaders. Consequently, instead of unity, Ukraine experienced prolonged strife and bloodshed during the seventeenth and the eighteenth centuries.

In the eighteenth century the Uniate church in the Polish-Lithuanian Commonwealth received two benefits. Early in the century several Orthodox dioceses in Galicia and Volyn joined the Uniates, and in 1720 the Uniate Church was officially recognized as an independent ecclesiastic entity within the Roman Catholic Church. And late in the century, as a result of the three partitions of the Polish-Lithuanian Commonwealth, Ukrainian Uniates of Galicia found themselves under Austrian jurisdiction. Austrian Catholic authorities showed a benevolent attitude towards the Uniates who, in turn, responded with deep loyalty. During the reigns of Maria Theresa and Joseph II, the Church's name was officially changed from Uniate to Greek Catholic (thus pro-forma equal to Roman Catholic); and, to elevate the intellectual standards of the Uniate clergy, the Austrians organized two theological seminaries—one in Vienna, the other in Lvov. In 1807 Uniate status was further enhanced with the elevation of a Uniate bishop to Metropolitan of Galicia. This action made him the official spiritual leader of the Ukrainian Uniates, defender of their rights, and their chief spokesman. That action also made the Greek Catholic Church the national church of Galician Ukrainians.

Progress was slow, however, because in Galicia, as throughout Austria, the church hierarchy reflected the conservative outlook of the era of Metternich. Still, change came thanks to the efforts of many dedicated young Uniate priests who, influenced by the spirit of romanticism and liberalism, published their works in the language of the people, encouraged them to become literate, advocated the expansion of elementary schools, organized a printing press, the first Ukrainian newspaper, reading clubs, village cooperatives, and promoted such populist ideas as temperance, self-reliance, gymnastics, choirs, amateur theatrical groups, and Ukrainian national consciousness. In short, through its clergy, the Greek Catholic Church in Galicia spearheaded the birth of modern Ukrainian nationhood.

These activities had three far-reaching repercussions. First, they alienated many conservatives, who (with generous support from Russian authorities) turned to Russophilism and even tried to invent a new language, known as *iazychie* (or patois), an incomprehensible mixture of Church Slavonic, Ukrainian, and Russian. Its intent was to block the elevation of Ukrainian as the literary language. Second, the populist campaign against drunkenness among peasants antagonized many nobles (because it deprived them of revenues) and led to the dismissal of several radical Greek Catholic priests. Finally, although it was slow in coming, the Greek Catholic-sponsored activity made possible the emergence of Ukrainian lay intelligentsia and the founding of Ukrainian political parties. It should be noted that the Greek Catholic Church benefited enormously from the activities of the Basilian monks who, after 1882, concentrated their energies on improving elementary and secondary education and on raising the educational level of the masses.

The most forceful spokesman of the Ukrainian Greek Catholic Church in the twentieth century was Metropolitan Andrew Sheptyckii

(1864-1944). A descendant of an old, but Polonized, Ukrainian noble family, Sheptyckii was involved in many activities during his long service as Metropolitan. He advocated ecumenical movement among the churches, founded new theological seminaries, sent the most capable theological students to study abroad, reorganized monastic orders, expressed interest in the spiritual needs of Ukrainian emigrants in the Western Hemisphere, generously supported Ukrainian cultural, educational, humanitarian, and economic institutions, and encouraged the Greek Catholic clergy to become involved in community life. These activites created for Sheptyckii innumerable problems. Ukrainian extremists accused him of not being fully committed to Ukrainian nationalism. Imperial Russian authorities arrested and deported him to Siberia in 1915 for being too pro-Ukrainian. From 1918 to 1939 Polish authorities harassed him for harboring an anti-Polish bias. During their brief control of Galicia Nazi officials kept an attentive vigil over his activities; and the Soviets carefully monitored all of his moves.

Under Sheptyckii's guidance the Ukrainian Greek Catholic Church, as an institution, made enormous strides. It published numerous journals and newpapers; operated many elementary and secondary schools, monasteries, nunneries and several theological seminaries; acquired substantial real estate; and organized youth and adult organizations (for both men and women), reading clubs, and cooperatives. On the eve of World War II, in Poland alone the Church had some 2,500 parishes, 3,660 churches, 3,000 priests, and 3,600,000 faithful. Outside Poland (i.e., in Western Europe and the Western Hemisphere) the Ukrainian Greek Catholic Church had many followers and pursued similar activities.

Many members of the Ukrainian Greek Catholic Church paid a heavy price for its successes. At the end of World War I, for example, Polish authorities arrested many priests for their alleged support of Ukrainian efforts to establish Ukrainian administration in Galicia. Subsequently, Polish authorities discriminated against Ukrainian Greek Catholics, treated them as second-class Christians, attempted to Polonize the Lemko region of Galicia, and, after World War II, tortured and executed many Ukrainian Greek Catholic priests and faithful for alleged involvement in the Ukrainian national movement. Soviet and Czechoslovak authorities behaved in a like manner in their respective jurisdictions. And, as noted earlier, on Stalin's orders the Ukrainian Greek Catholic Church was officially dissolved and ceased to exist under Soviet control in March, 1946. Stalin's order did not affect Ukrainian Greek Catholic communities in Western Europe, Canada, the United States, Latin America, Australia, and other regions where Ukrainians have settled. The Church there not only exists but flourishes as well.

In a number of ways the Ukrainian Orthodox Church matched the misfortunes of its Greek Catholic counterpart. In both instances the principal cause was the absence of an independent Ukrainian state capable of protecting them. Between 1654 and 1795 the Ukrainian Orthodox found themselves under two foreign jurisdictions: Polish and Russian. Those under Polish rule experienced increased attention and intervention on their behalf by Russian political and religious authorities. Accordingly, Polish Roman Catholic authorities considered Ukrainian Orthodox to be traitors and subjected them to increased suspicion and harassment. This no-win situation stemmed from the rapidly declining fortunes of Poland, the sudden rise of Imperial Russia as a major power in Europe, and the inability of Polish leaders to include in the numerous agreements with the Russians a provision that would, technically at least, prevent Russian interference on behalf of the Orthodox. Instead of protecting their countless Orthodox subjects (Ukrainian and Belorussian), the Poles resorted to a policy of discrimination. Consequently, although she was not a religious person, Catherine II responded positively to appeals by a few Ukrainian Orthodox spokesmen to protect them against Polish Roman Catholic persecution. These appeals contributed substantially to Russia's participation in the three partitions of the Polish-Lithuanian Common-wealth that placed all Ukrainians under Russian rule, except those living in Galicia, Bukovina, Eastern Slovakia, and in present-day *Zakarpatska oblast'* of the UkSSR.

Those Orthodox Ukrainians who lived under Imperial Russian rule from the middle of the seventeenth century also experienced ever-increasing supervision and harassment by Russian authorities. Space will not allow the listing of all such measures. The following are a few samples of Russian centralizing steps aimed at controlling the Ukrainian Orthodox Church in the seventeenth and eighteenth centuries. In 1685 the Russians masterminded the election of the Metropolitan of Kiev (who was then consecrated in Moscow) as the spiritual head of Orthodox Ukrainians. Early in the eighteenth century they placed several dioceses of the Ukrainian Orthodox Church under the jurisdiction of Moscow's religious authorities. After 1721, following the establishment of the Holy Synod, all Russian rulers reserved to themselves the right to appoint all high ecclesiastic leaders (in the Ukraine as well as throughout the empire). In subsequent years, as an intergral part of imperial centralizing measures over all aspects of life, the tsar assumed the right to appoint all abbots, secularized all church and monastic properities, and, in Ukraine, imposed a systematic Russification policy on the Ukrainian Orthodox Church.

During the nineteenth century Imperial Russian authorities russified theological education in Ukraine by introducing Russian pronunciation into the reading of liturgical texts and encouraging use of the Russian language in sermons. They also appointed Russian-born priests to Ukrainian parishes, sent uncooperative Ukrainian-born priests into Russia's interior, forced all priests in the Ukraine to grow long beards, and pressured the clergy (secular and monastic) to participate actively in Russian political organizations of the extreme right. Moreover, they banned the church brotherhoods, discontinued the use of old Ukrainian ceremonies associated with baptism and marriage, and outlawed lay involvement in church matters. They likewise censored all Ukrainian publications, prescribed architectural styles for new churches, and suppressed local traditions of icon painting. Finally, they forbade publication of the Bible in the Ukrainian language for fear that it would somehow contribute to the creation of an independent Ukrainian state. These and many other uncivilized measures continued unabated until the revolution of 1917.

The collapse of the imperial regime in March, 1917, opened a new chapter in the history of the Ukrainian Orthodox Church. Emboldened by the appearance of political autonomy centered around the Rada government, there emerged in the Ukraine a religious movement that demanded Ukrainization of the Church and its complete independence from Moscow. This demand was not realized because it was opposed by the strategically-placed Russian-dominated church hierarchy and because, in spite of many efforts, the Ukrainians failed to sustain a viable independent government that would defend this demand. Instead of gaining political independence, which, in turn, would assure its religious independence, for over three years Ukraine experienced bloody revolutionary turmoil and military invasions by the Bolshivik, German, Austro-Hungarian, White Russian, and Polish forces. When Soviet forces gained full control of the Ukraine in 1920, the Ukrainian Orthodox Church had two bodies: the Russian Patriarchal Church presided over by an Exarch controlled by the Russian Patriarch in Moscow and by Soviet authorities; and the Ukrainian Autocephalous Church, headed by the Metropolitan of Kiev, that embraced nationally-conscious believers. In 1923 there appeared on the scene an officially-supported third body—the Living Church—which also was headed by a metropolitan.

The three churches faced an uphill struggle, partly because they quarreled among themselves, but, mostly, because Soviet authorities in Moscow imposed numerous restrictions on their activities and terrorized their followers. In the mid-1920s almost all spokesmen of the Russian Patriarchal Church in the Ukraine were arrested and prevented from resuming their posts until they pledged unconditional loyalty to the Soviet state. In the subsequent anti-church terror conducted by Stalin, Soviet authorities arrested practically all bishops and priests and closed most churches, monasteries, and nunneries. The Ukrainian Auto-cephalous Church experienced the same fate. In the 1930s Stalin dissolved it and exterminated its leaders and countless of its followers. It should be noted that during its brief existence, the Ukrainian Autocephalous Church was able to establish a presence among Ukrainians living in Western Europe and in the Western Hemisphere which it maintains to the present day. In the 1930s also, Stalin meted out brutal treatment to members of the Living Church.

During and since World War II Soviet authorities altered somewhat their treatment of all religions in the USSR and, perhaps because of their sheer numbers, have singled out the Russian Orthodox for special consideration. This change of attitude stemmed primarily from the regime's dire need to gain popular support in its war effort and from some pressures from abroad. They lifted some restrictions on the activities of the Church, allowed the reopening of some churches, theological seminaries, and monasteries, and approved the election of the Patriarch. However, to insure control of the Church's activities, the Soviets established a Committee within the Council of Ministers at the end of 1943 which still exists today and which, in accordance with a centuries-old tradition, enforces political control over the Russian Orthodox Church. This has enabled the Russian Patriarch of Moscow to establish jurisdiction over Ukrainians living in Galicia, Bukovina, and the Zakarpatska oblast', i.e., regions that the Soviet Union annexed at the end of World War II. In those regions the Patriarch either dissolved or made impossible the existence of other churches regardless of their professions or affiliations. It should be noted that, to commemorate the millennium of Christianity, Soviet authorities have made numerous, albeit trivial, concessions to their Orthodox subjects. Only time will tell whether these concessions are genuine and lasting or simply pragmatic and timely.

In spite of nearly insurmountable obstacles and interferences the Ukrainian Orthodox Church also managed to exist in Poland before World War II. Its activities there were subjected to numerous restrictions. The Poles viewed Orthodox Ukrainians as traitors, closed many of their churches and schools, and promulgated a law that granted the state the power to appoint and dismiss all religious officials and to introduce Polish as the official language of the Church. Because Ukrainians resisted these measures the authorities applied intimidation, terror, and destruction. When these measures failed to accomplish the desired results, the authorities forced many Orthodox Ukrainians to embrace Roman Catholicism and destroyed many of their churches. In short, Polish treatment of Ukrainian Christians, regardless of whether they were Greek Catholic or Orthodox, was uncivilized.

This brief survey of the history of the Ukrainian church has brought forth the following conclusions. First, because they have been unable to establish an independent Ukrainian state on a prolonged and sustained basis, the Ukrainians (Orthodox as well as Greek Catholic) have, over centuries, paid a very high price for their religious convictions. Second, Russian authorities (tsarist and communist) have distrusted, discriminated against, and brutalized the Ukrainians for their beliefs. Third, Polish officials (Roman Catholic and communist) have mistreated and often terrorized the Ukrainians for their convictions. And, fourth, many Ukrainians in recent years have managed to leave their homeland for Western Europe, Canada, the United States, Latin America, and Australia, where they have either continued to adhere to the faith of their ancestors, or have been free to join various Protestant denominations, or to become Christian dropouts.

SELECTED BIBLIOGRAPHY

Bohdan R. Bociurkiw, "The Politics of Religion in the Ukraine: The Orthodox Church and the Ukrainian Revolution, 1917-1919." Washington: Kennan Institute for Advanced Russian Studies. *Occasional Paper* #202.

Bohdan Buchynskii, "Zmahaniia do unii ruskoi tserkvi z Rymom v rokakh 1498-1506." *Zapysky Ukrainskoho Tovarystva v Kievi.* Kiev: 1909, vols. IV, V, VI.

(Metropolitan) Makarii Bulgakov, *Istoriia russkoi tserkvi.* St. Petersburg: 1879-1898. 12 vols.

"The Destruction of the Ukrainian Catholic Church in the Soviet Union." *Prologue* (New York), vol. 4, Nos. 1–2 (Spring-Summer, 1960).

Evgenii E. Golubinskii, *Istoriia russkoi tserkvi.* Moscow: 1901. 2 vols.

John-Paul Himka, *The Greek Catholic Church and Ukrainian Society in Austrian Galicia.* Cambridge: Harvard University Ukrainian Studies Fund, 1987.

Oskar Halecki, *From Florence to Brest.* Rome: Sacrum Poloniae Millennium, 1958.

George C. Jerkovich, *A Thousand Years of Russian Christianity: Kievan Rus' to Present. Comments and a Survey of the Literature.* Lawrence: University of Kansas Press, 1988.

Vasyl Lypikivskii, *Istoriia ukrainskoi pravoslavnoi tserkvi.* Winnipeg: 1961.

"Millennium of Christianity in Kievan Rus'-Ukraine, 988-1988." *Smoloskyp,* vol. 8, Nos. 38-39 (Summer-Fall, 1988).

Ihor Moncar, *Florentine Ecumenism in the Kyivan Church.* Rome: Ukrainian Catholic University, 1987.

Julian Pelesz, *Geschichte der Union der Ruthenischen Kirche mit Rom.* Vienna: 1872. 2 vols.

Paul Pierling, S. J., *La Russie et le Saint-Siège.* Paris: 1896. 5 vols.

Ihor Sevcenko, *Byzantine Roots of Ukrainian Christianity.* Cambridge: Harvard University Ukrainian Studies Fund, 1984.

Frank E. Sysyn, *The Ukrainian Orthodox Question in the USSR.* Cambridge: Harvard University Ukrainian Studies Fund, 1987.

"The Ukrainian Church." *Ukraine: A Concise Encyclopedia.* Toronto: University of Toronto Press, 1963. Vol. 2, pp. 120-231.

Atanasii H. Velykii, *Narys istorii ukrainskoi pravoslavnoi tserkvi.* New York: 1955–56. 4 vols.

Osyp Zinkewych and Andrew Sorokowski, eds. *A Thousand Years of Christianity in Ukraine: An Encyclopedic Chronology.* New York: Smoloskyp Publishers, 1988.

6

Christianity and Russia in the Modern Era

Donald W. Treadgold
University of Washington

To start with, a few basic facts. The religion of the Rus', the ancestors of the Ukrainians, Belorussians, and Great Russians, for 1,000 years has been Eastern Orthodoxy, which traces its ancestry back to the very beginnings of Christianity, and is a product of Greek churches, whose senior prelate is the Patriarch of Constantinople, today Istanbul, and whose other highest ecclesiastical authorities are the patriarchs of Alexandria, Antioch, and Jerusalem, though all four of these patriarchs, in the size of their flocks and their influence, are but a pale reflection of the days when their followers were numbered in the millions, before the Muslim conquest of Asia Minor, Syria, Egypt, and the rest of North Africa.

In the late seventeenth century occurred the only schism ever in the history of Russian Orthodoxy: the Old Believers, a colony of whom is in Woodburn, Oregon, broke off, and still survive with possibly one million in the Soviet Union.[1] Other Christian groups with shadowy beginnings but probably dating from the eighteenth century called sectarians, as distinct from schismatics, include the Dukhobors (who are well represented in Western Canada), Molokane, Khlysty, and Skoptsy, some of whom may be influenced by the West. The Baptists, who are a Western importation, of which there may be two million, represent the fusion in 1944 of Evangelical Christians or Pashkovtsy, followers of Colonel Pashkov who introduced sectarians into aristocratic circles near the end of the nineteenth century, and Baptists who emerged about the same time among the peasants of the Ukraine. One interesting feature of the Baptists is the Initiative Group that formed its own organ in 1964–65, and is outside the law without being unequivocally banned. Legalized Baptists benefit from the existence of such a group, for the government knows that, if pressure on them grows too great, some will defect to the Initiative

Group or *initsiativniki*. Many Westerners are taken to the single Protestant church, which is Baptist, operating in Moscow today for a service full of singing and weeping, leading to some mistaken impressions that foreigners carry away. There are 600 Roman Catholic parishes in Lithuania, and a sizable percent of the population in Latvia is also Roman Catholic, yet there are very few Russians who are Roman Catholic. There were almost no Jews in medieval Muscovy; but, with the annexation of Polish territories by Catherine II in the late eighteenth century, a large number of Jews came into the Russian empire, a culture described in *Fiddler on the Roof.* Today there may be possibly two million Jews, of whom possibly 250,000 are religious practicing Jews. There have been Muslims in the USSR from way back. The Mongols, who conquered Russia in 1240, were originally pagans converted to Islam, but large Muslim territories were brought in only with the annexation of Central Asia in the late nineteenth century. In 1917 there were 25,000 mosques, but today there are fewer than 500 mosques for 45 million Muslims.

But today I shall concentrate on Russian Orthodoxy, the historic faith of the Russians, in our time becoming an increasingly significant factor in the lives of Russians. I shall try to identify several issues that have been significant under tsarist and Soviet rule and try to give you some perspective on Orthodoxy in Russia today. The position of Orthodoxy has changed a good deal, and more than once. It is often difficult to remember that these changes have occurred. If one compares Russia's position with Poland's, one is apt to think of Poland, which today is approximately 96% Roman Catholic, religiously homogeneous, and extraordinarily fervent, as always having been that way. However, in the sixteenth century much of Poland, perhaps most of the Polish population, became Calvinist and Unitarian before the Counter-Reformation reclaimed them for Roman Catholicism, and the depth of belief has increased since then. The United States was a Christian country half a century ago, and one need not describe what it is today, for these things change. Do not be misled by the fact that Pat Robertson carried the Washington caucuses, Washington has the least amount of churches of all the states, and Oregon has only a few more.

Western countries including the United States have had little experience with Eastern Christianity, and they have little knowledge of Christianity in Russia, especially Russian Orthodoxy. In World War II it was possible to be "C" for Catholic, "P" for Protestant, or "J" for Jewish, and to have these letters respectively entered on one's dogtags. I believe that they now permit one to be "O" for Orthodox, which is not to be confused with the blood type. Even scholarly accounts until recently have been unsympathetic to Orthodoxy, perhaps on the basis of Puritan hostility to art, decoration, indeed the material side of life. Puritanism left traces in American consciousness even after the "last Puritan," to use George Santayana's phrase, was long dead, perhaps simply because Russian Orthodoxy seemed foreign, alien, and mysterious. An example of an early post-World War I publication, based on a pre-revolutionary study by F. C. Conybeare, states: "The official Church is dead, exhausted, under the thumb of lay bureaucrats ... the religious life of Orthodoxy is reduced to a legalistic formalism." [2]

On the other hand, recent reports from American clergymen who were able to visit the Soviet Union have been upbeat and positive, indicating that Christianity is not only alive in the Soviet Union, but enjoys religious freedom, as do all faiths. However, these reports are inaccurate. Many of those who make them do not begin to understand what it means for a government to be officially atheist and committed to the extinction of religion. For a church to try to survive in such a country is not easy, and those who make such reports are simply uninformed.

The complexity of the religious situation in Russia cannot be reduced to any simple formula. The strength of religious belief today is great and deep among Russians, who make up only about half of the Soviet population (though if one adds Ukrainians and Belorussians, this will comprise an additional quarter for a total of three fourths of the population). A much-quoted Soviet literary publication, *Krokodil,* noted that: "All Russians are Christians. They always have been and always will be." (20 June, 1962) This is obviously an exaggeration, but it draws on truth, for it was a thousand years ago that the Eastern Slavs or Rus' (the term Russians came later), accepted Christianity. In that period of time faith may take root in a people, in contrast to the situation in the Pacific Northwest, where Christianity was brought by Caucasians to the Indians, along with themselves, only a little over a century ago. So let us try to single out a few issues for closer examination.

First, with respect to the ordinary individual's contact with the church, laymen, and laywomen, the attitude of the ordinary worshipper toward the Orthodox Church before the Revolution was apt to be reserved. The parish clergy did not always merit respect, and high clerics were often lumped with high officials, who were often one and the same. After the revolution, the situation changed markedly; the visit of the newly elected patriarch Tikhon to Petrograd in May, 1918, was a triumph, and he, standing up in his carriage for miles, blessed enormous crowds. This is one reason why it is forbidden for a priest to appear on the street in clerical garb today in the Soviet Union.

Before the Russian Revolution frequent communion was unknown in the Russian Orthodox Church. Only Father John of Kronstadt preached that it was necessary, but today it is common among believers. However, with or without communion, Russians have always loved the liturgy. Even hostile observers are not entirely immune to its beauty. Alfred Rosenberg, Hitler's assistant for non-Russian peoples, called the Orthodox service an "oriental custom with nice songs." [3] It was he who was permitted by Hitler to issue in June of 1942 a Toleration Act permitting the population to practice their religion. Father Louis Bouyer declares the Orthodox liturgy one of the greatest creations of Christian civilization, if not the greatest, and theologians and laity alike hold that with the help of icons, murals, and acappella choral singing the Orthodox service is heaven brought to earth.

Currently, the Soviet constitution guarantees freedom of religious worship and anti-religious propaganda, but no religious "propaganda," that is, any kind of defense of Christianity whatever, is permitted. Moreover, freedom of religious worship is in fact severely restricted. If one is observed attending a church service, a person may suffer discrimination of all kinds. If he is a member of the *Komsomol*, he must be severely reprimanded even though it is recognized that there are what is called in Russian *komsomoltsy-bogomoltsy*, that is, Young Communists who pray to God and who must be punished and prevented from such behavior in the future.

There are rituals, however, that are intended as a substitute for church sacraments weddings in the marriage palaces, registration of children in lieu of baptism, memorial meetings instead of church funerals but these are scorned and avoided by many. The ordinary person may dare to attend the liturgy on Sundays or other holy days, be married by a priest, bring his baby in, preferably when not being observed, for baptism, and may have the good fortune of having a church funeral at his or her death. The persistence of religious belief in an officially atheist society, and specifically of religious ceremonies, is quite amazing. Nikita Struve estimates that in the mid-1960s about 100 million out of 160 million babies of Orthodox descent were baptized in the USSR. Until 1928 almost all newborn babies among Russians were baptized. The generation between 1928 and 1944 felt the worst effects of the physical annihilation of the church and had the fewest number of baptisms. A 1955 study of a marshy region, which is difficult to approach, the area of Zagalie, in the district of Luban, showed that almost all of the young people were baptized. Yet the nearest working church was eighteen miles away, and there was no transportation available except for cars belonging to the collective farm or *kolkhoz*, or to villagers who were not particularly devout.[4] Not just believers, but all the parents, wanted their children baptized why? Astonishing reasons were given: parents feared that their children would reproach them if they were not baptized, it was a national tradition, and so on. There were fewer baptisms performed in larger towns. In the mid-1950s in Sverdlovsk about 30% of the children were baptized, but in Moscow they numbered 50%. Today perhaps 50% of babies among the Russians are baptized.[5] About 60% of the dead are buried with a church funeral. There is reason to think that there are about 50 million Orthodox believers in the Soviet Union today, although church membership is not an appropriate category.[6]

A second issue for examination is the legal position of the church. In 1721 the church was reduced to an arm of the state; the clergy were even supposed to report anti-state activity they learned about in the confessional, though this controverted the canons and was widely disobeyed. It was a paradox in which Orthodoxy constituted the official state church that was given unambiguous preference over other faiths, but was still subject to direct government control. This paradox was especially glaring after 1905 when schismatics, Old Believers, and sectarians were granted full religious freedom, but the Orthodox remained under the Holy Synod. In 1917, after repeatedly requests in vain for official permission to convene a council and regain its independence from the state, the Church did so on its own initiative when the tsar was overthrown. This council restored freedom for diocesan clergy and laity to elect bishops, decided to strengthen monastic education, gave women various roles in the church, and was about to restore the ancient order of deaconesses when the council had to disperse.

The earliest Soviet legislation separated church and state, except that they were not actually separated. The church was still confined in a series of ways, this time by an atheist state, and not by the semi-Christian state of the tsars. The Church in the USSR cannot own property. From the earliest Soviet legislation the *dvadtsatka,* or twenty laymen, were permitted to lease and use buildings including churches. In 1929 all charitable work was prohibited as were all forms of social action. The clergy were stripped of ration cards and the right to medical care. The law of August, 1929, eliminated observance of Sunday by instituting the continuous work week, without a common rest day. Ever since there has been little freedom of religious worship and intensification of anti-religious propaganda. During the next five to six years, thousands of churches were destroyed, almost fifty churches and monasteries in Moscow alone. Bellringing was forbidden and the bells were melted down. The Church of the Savior in Moscow was destroyed to be replaced by the Palace of the Soviets. When the foundations sank, the project was given up and a swimming pool was built, now used for performing baptisms.

There have been several periods of direct attack on the Church. First, from 1918 to 1923, Lenin took the opportunity to attack the church directly, in connection with the state demand for consecrated articles during the famine of 1921. In February, 1922, he signed an order that the next party Congress should organize jointly with the GPU, the Commissariat of Justice, and the Revolution Tribunal in a secret session to approve a "mercilessly resolute" confiscation of church valuables. According to Lenin, "The more members of the reactionary bourgeoisie we manage to shoot the better. It is precisely now that we must give such a lesson to these characters that they would not dare to think of any resistance for at least the next few decades." Over 8,000 priests, monks, and nuns were killed in 1922 alone.[7] This was also the year of the trial of Metropolitan Benjamin of Petrograd, who was defended by the Jewish lawyer Gurovich.

He paid tribute to the attitude of the Russian Orthodox clergy during the Beilis case of 1913. The metropolitan was executed with three others.

The second period of attack on the church came during the Stalin persecution 1928 to 1939. A good estimate is that about 42,000 Orthodox clergy were killed from the beginning of the regime through this period.[8] In 1941 the number of working churches on pre-1939 Soviet territory was under 1,000, as against almost 50,000 at the time of the Russian Revolution. There were almost no bishops functioning, and overt Christianity was almost extinct in Russia.

The third period came with the Khrushchev persecution during 1959–64. Preparations began in 1957 for a world congress of 350 atheistic militants, to discuss the influence of religion on youth and old women. To cover itself, the regime then authorized the Moscow Patriarchate to publish a book in seven languages, in 1961, depicting the state of the church as flourishing. Then a widespread closing of churches took place between 1959-61. Often, a priest's registration was canceled or he was arrested. When this occurred, a new *dvadtsatka* had to be elected by the parish. Yet, this could not be accomplished without the permission of the local Party committee, and more often than not this was denied. The churches, then, were not used, and the government would order church keys to be given up. The wholesale destruction of churches never stopped throughout this period. The cathedral of Ufa, the oldest building in the city, was blown up in 1956, and a twelfth century church in Vitebsk was demolished in 1961. Monasteries were closed. When a 97-year-old monk came at the Patriarch's order to live at Pochaev in the West, he was seized by the police, interrogated for a whole week, and then asked to leave. *Krokodil* jeered at the monks at Pochaev because, it said, the icy temperature of the cells interfered with communication with the Most High. This is akin to the vulgar atheist claim that since airplane pilots and cosmonauts have not seen God in the sky, there is no God—of course, if God proved to have material being, that would support materialism, and not religion.

The third issue to address is the Church and education. Before the Revolution, the best Russian seminaries and the more advanced academies were on an extremely high intellectual level. From 1918 to 1944, the church was permitted no intellectual life at all. All ecclesiastical schools were closed, although eight seminaries and two academies were restored in the late 1940's. In Khrushchev's persecution of religion up to 1964, five out of the eight seminaries were closed, and the number of students remaining was reduced, often by drafting into the army those wishing to become priests. Three seminaries and two academies, in Zagorsk and Leningrad, are still operating. A four-year course is available in the seminaries, with four more years available to the more gifted students in the academies. The curriculum is evidently not strong: after 1958, no philosophical subject at all has been offered. One must start from the beginning in explaining Christianity: in 1986, out of the 400 students at the Leningrad Theological Academy and Seminary, 70% were from secular or actively atheistic families. Education may push toward conversion in unlikely ways. In the case of Aleksandr Ogorodnikov, he was a student in the Moscow Institute of Cinematography, when he saw Pasolini's film, *The Gospel According to St Matthew,* and became interested in Christianity. Ogorodnikov became not merely a convert, but also a leader of a Christian seminar. He was arrested, and only recently released. Many cannot get admitted to seminaries, but there are other routes. By the end of 1980, 1,100 students were studying to become priests by correspondence.

The fourth issue to consider is the relationship between the Church and monasticism. It may be difficult for a Westerner who is apt to think a contemplative life odd, or possibly morally reprehensible on the grounds of laziness, to grasp how important monks and nuns were in Russian life before the Revolution. In 1917 there were 1,025 monasteries and convents in the Russian Empire. Today there are only six monasteries and ten convents, the most famous being the Monastery of the Trinity and St. Sergius, at Zagorsk, which houses about ninety monks, of whom half are priests. The largest convent is the Pokrovsky convent at Kiev, housing about 200 nuns. Only one convent, in Odessa, has been founded since 1917. All attract pilgrims, who are often harassed by the militia.

The present situation of the Orthodox Church dates from 1943. Though Stalin had virtually wiped out the visible church in Russia, when the German invasion came it underwent an amazing and universal resuscitation behind German lines. On the Soviet side, the senior cleric Metropolitan Sergii placed himself unambiguously on the side of the Red Army from June 22, 1941, and rallied many clergy and laity to do the same. There ensued a remarkable scene when Sergii and others were called to the Kremlin at night and were told that they could hold another council and elect a patriarch, for there had been none since the death of Tikhon in 1925, and enjoy other privileges. Stalin asked Sergii where his cadres were, but Stalin should have known for it was he who destroyed them. Sergii, in response, took a deep breath and said that there were many reasons, one being that we put a man through the seminary and, instead of becoming a priest, he became Marshal of the Soviet Union. Stalin loved the answer. Since then Sergii, Aleksii, and Pimen, as patriarchs, have been compelled to follow the line which Dimitry Pospielovsky characterizes as inheriting the worst of both preceding worlds: "the extreme conservatism of the prerevolutionary official Orthodoxy and the sycophancy ... of Renovationalism" [9] that is, the leftist movement within the clergy and laity in the early 1920s, not created by Communist infiltration but strongly supported by the Communist government as a way of weakening the church as long as it seemed to have any chance of attracting real support, and cast aside after that. Pospielovsky is right that there was indeed extreme conservatism and a strongly reactionary element in official Orthodoxy before the revolution, but it is too sweeping a statement to suggest that that was all, for there were reformers and radicals among the clergy, some of whom were elected as deputies to the Duma. But Pospielovsky is generally right nevertheless about the line that the hierarchy of the church must follow today.

That is the current situation of the Russian Orthodox Church in the Soviet Union. Church leaders avoid any taint of modernism of any sort, like the Roman Catholic church in the People's Republic of China which still insists on using Latin in the liturgy. The leaders of the Russian Orthodox Church avoid anything but strictly religious activity in the Soviet Union, yet in foreign and international contexts it defends Soviet foreign policy, but this is the price paid for survival. This does not assure the safety of the priests who interpret these principles broadly, for there are still hundreds of "prisoners of conscience," a number of whom are in psychiatric hospitals receiving painful and damaging "injections" for mental troubles they do not have. The *Keston College News* regularly carries stories of suffering and martyrdom of individual clerics. The ordinary people of Russia understand very well the complexities of the situation. They hail bishops, venerate monks, and continue to believe despite pressures to which Western visitors are blind.

A Soviet Russian priest told Pospielovsky: "What the western churches are going through now we experienced in the 1920s, and we are just beginning to recover from their effects," [10] referring to the leftist resolutions, the consecration of priests and bishops who doubt Christian creeds and seek in every way to adopt the the *Zeitgeist*, or spirit of the age. In our time the Russian Orthodox Church has suffered immense damage from direct and indirect attacks by the atheist Soviet government and, in a different way, by the misunderstanding and misinformation of Westerners, clerical and lay. But today the Church is reaffirming its Christian beliefs, its reverence toward its own saints and sinners of the past, its vocation in its search for God. All this is attracting many, including the young, who have lost faith in Marxism and seek another path. In other words, there are advantages to persecution, which the Russian Orthodox Church continues to enjoy. Its situation is not so different from the church in the Roman Empire of the first and second centuries, in which there were suffering and martyrdom, but also deep belief and a growing if still modest-sized church. Those of us who believe in freedom and freedom of religion as an important aspect of it wish that it may survive and prosper.

NOTES

1. Trevor Beeson, *Discretion and Valour: Religious Conditions in Russia and Eastern Europe* (Philadelphia: Fortress Press, 1982), gives a good survey of all faiths in the countries concerned.

2. Frederick C. Conybeare, *Russian Dissenters* (Cambridge: Harvard University Press, 1962 [1921]), pp. 256-57. These statements, in context, seem to summarize Old Believers' views, but the whole book suggests that the author shares them.

3. Dimitry Pospielovsky, *The Russian Church Under the Soviet Regime, 1917-1982* (Crestwood, NY: St. Vladimir's Seminary Press, 1984), I:25, quoting but also correcting Harvey Fireside's *Icon and Swastika.*

4. Nikita Struve, *Christians in Contemporary Russia,* translated from second edition (New York: Charles Scribner's Sons, 1967), p. 177.

5. Gerald Buss, *The Bear's Hug* (London: Hodder & Stoughton, 1987), p. 60.

6. Struve, p. 180.
7. *Ibid.*, p. 38.
8. Hutten, *Iron Curtain Christians,* as quoted in Buss, p. 28.
9. *Ibid.*, I:92.
10. *Ibid.*, p. 87.

Dissent and Conformity in the Russian Orthodox Church, 1943–1988

Robert L. Nichols

St. Olaf College

I

For westerners, understanding modern Orthodoxy is often made difficult by the lack of sound information and proper perspective. Recently, for example, *Time* magazine wrote of the Russian church that, "after centuries of training in servility, most Orthodox leaders have nothing but praise for the Soviet treatment of religion." [*Time*, April 4, 1988, pp. 64–5] This characterization is inaccurate both about earlier centuries as well as about the Orthodox hierarchy in the Soviet era. Metropolitan Filip in the sixteenth century, Patriarch Nikon in the seventeenth, Arsenii of Rostov in the eighteenth, and Filaret of Moscow in the nineteenth are readily cited examples of hierarchs who spoke out, defending the church and faithful against unwarranted state intrusion in the life of the church. Patriarch Tikhon, after his election amidst the Soviet revolution of 1917, showed great courage in trying to avert the "new Russian martyrdom" that overwhelmed the church in the 1920s and 1930s, a period of state sponsored schism and persecution whose severity and duration is perhaps unprecedented in the history of Christianity. A sobering realization of what the new order meant for the Orthodox hierarchy can be gained merely by paging through the list of arrested, killed, and unaccounted for bishops compiled in Lev Regel'son's remarkable book *The Tragedy of the Russian Church*. In 1917, Orthodoxy had several hundred bishops; by 1939 only four still held office, a few more were in retirement or wardens of churches, and some had died of natural causes. But the vast majority were killed or imprisoned. Thus, it is wrong to suggest that "most Orthodox leaders have nothing but praise for the Soviet treatment of religion," as *Time* contends.

The Soviet Revolution aimed at a complete removal of Christian life from Soviet society.

The outbreak of the Second World War and the timely actions of Metropolitan Sergii, the caretaker of the office of the patriarch after Tikhon's death in 1925, unexpectedly gave Orthodoxy the opportunity to reenter the national life in a public way. Despite a large literature to the contrary, the new opportunity did not arise from any initiative from Stalin, who, it is sometimes said, suddenly remembered the Orthodox church and summoned Sergii to the Kremlin to work out a new church-state concordat. Rather, Metropolitan Sergii publicly appealed to the nation on the very next day after the German invasion, June 22, 1941, the feastday of All the Saints of Russia, declaring that "Our Orthodox Church has always shared in the destinies of the nation ... Together with it she has borne both trials and successes. Neither shall she abandon her people today. She is giving this impending national struggle the heavenly bless-ings." It took another two years of appeals to patriotism and to "the great faith of the Russian people in God's help to the just cause" in the war before Stalin's hostility toward the church began to abate. In January 1943 Sergii illegally, but with Stalin's permission to his request, opened a bank account in the name of the Russian Orthodox church as the church's Fund for the Defense of the Country. Within ten days, 3.2 million rubles were collected for the fund in the besieged and starving Leningrad alone, plus another half million rubles for a tank column named after Dmitrii Donskoi, the fourteenth-century Orthodox victor over the Mongols. By October 1944 total church donations reached 150 million rubles. It was these actions by Sergii and the church which led directly to Stalin's celebrated meeting with Sergii in the Kremlin in September 1943, where Sergii asked Stalin for the mass reopening of churches, the convocation of a church council and the election of a patriarch, and seminaries to train clergy.

"And why don't you have cadres?" Stalin asked. "Where have they disappeared?"

Sergii replied, "There are all sorts of reasons why we have no cadres. One of the reasons is that we train a person for the priesthood, and he becomes Marshal of the Soviet Union."

From that moment, Sergii's strategy of loyalty and prayer—conformity if you like—brought a steady improvement for Russian Orthodoxy that continued into the postwar years. The requests made by Sergii were granted, and a new statute for the Russian church was drafted legally recognizing its central administration, the patriarchate. As Soviet armies moved into German occupied areas, particularly the Ukraine, government authority was exercised in ways that benefited Russian Orthodoxy at the expense of the Ukrainian Orthodox church. The Uniate Church was declared illegal and its congregations forcibly reunited with the Russian church. After the war, the church continued to give strong support to Soviet foreign policy. By that time Patriarch Sergii was dead, succeeded in office by Patriarch Aleksii. Orthodox seminaries now graduated their first clergy, reflecting the patriarch's hope that these resurrected theological schools might truly be called "spiritual, where the learning of the pupils would be predominantly that of the spirit," a hope that was to have uncomfortable consequences for the central patriarchate in subsequent years.

II

Stalin's death in 1953 brought new and unexpected challenges which caught Orthodox leaders unprepared and showed the dangers from a too easy acceptance of the status quo of the late Stalin years. The challenges came from three directions: newly released Orthodox Christians from the Gulag; the rising younger generation of newly educated clergy and Orthodox laity; and Communist Party reformers led by Khrushchev, who were alarmed by the successes enjoyed by Orthodoxy and other Christian churches among Soviet young people. The new challenges were part of a widespread search for a moral alternative to the endless rationalizations for the expediency of state power during Stalin's lifetime. For the Communist Party the new era marked a period of religious persecution that restricted believers under a revised statute of 1961 governing church affairs.

Among the faithful, the new searching found examples and powerful testimony in the "saints" who returned from the wilderness of the Gulag in 1954 and 1955. Like Russia's earlier saints who returned to teach in the world after years of silence and suffering, these men and women bore witness to the power of the Holy Spirit that could inspire individuals in the face of the most inhumane cruelty. Accounts of brave suffering for

their faith by Orthodox inmates of labor camps imbued a younger generation with awe for those who endured. Evgeniia Ginzburg, herself not a
believer, provided moving testimony from her own labor camp experience:

> In that mortally dangerous spring, we were also much sustained by the strength
> of character shown by the semi-literate peasant women from Voronezh who had
> been sentenced for practicing their religion. Easter that year came at the end of
> April. Although they always filled their norm without any "window dressing"
> and it was largely thanks to them that the output plan for Kilometer 7 was
> fulfilled, Cousin [the camp director] wouldn't even listen to them when they
> begged to be excused from work for the first day of Easter. They had said that
> they would make up for it three times over.
>
> "We don't recognize any religious holidays here, and I won't stand for any
> subversion. Get out into the forest at once, and don't you try any of your tricks!
> If you do, you'll get a punishment you won't forget in a hurry!" And he gave
> precise instructions to his underlings.
>
> When the women refused to leave their hut, saying repeatedly, "It's Easter, it's
> Easter, it's a sin to work on Easter Day," they were driven out with rifle butts.
> When they got to the forest clearing they made a neat pile of their axes and saws,
> sat down quietly on the frozen tree stumps, and began to sing hymns. Thereupon
> the guards, evidently on instructions, ordered them to take off their shoes and
> stand barefoot in the icy water of one of the forest pools, which was still covered
> with a thin sheet of ice.

Of course, Aleksandr Solzhenitsyn became the best known of these
returning voices who prophesied that modern man—not just *Homo
Sovieticus* was in mortal danger of losing the righteousness rooted in
Christianity that the new industrial and materialist world explicitly repu-
diated. His famous short story of the selfless old woman Matryona ends
with the warning that without righteousness, no village, no city, no
country can stand. In this criticism Solzhenitsyn and others also included
the church leadership, not because it failed to protest against the regime
(such protests had shown that they would be suicidal for the church), but
because it had failed to pray for the victims. While bending the knee to
Caesar from necessity, the church had lost the righteousness that comes
from living in the Spirit and in truth. Solzhenitsyn's most dramatic effort
to raise this protest against the hierarchy came in 1971 in his so-called
"Lenten Letter" to the newly elected Patriarch Pimen protesting that
silence denied the church its only weapon: the truth.

By what reasoning is it possible to convince oneself that the planned destruction of the spirit and body of the church under the guidance of atheists is the best way of preserving it? Preserving it for whom? Certainly not for Christ. Preserving it by what means? By falsehood? But after the falsehood by whose hands are the holy sacraments to be celebrated? …Things were no easier at the birth of the Christian faith; nevertheless it held out and prospered. And showed us the way: sacrifice. Though deprived of all material strength, it is always victorious in sacrifice.

To the testimony of the prison camp returnees was soon added the voices of young clergy. Best known are two Moscow priests, Father Nikolai Eshliman and Father Gleb Iakunin, who addressed two open letters to the patriarch and to Nikolai Podgorny, then chairman of the Presidium of the Supreme Soviet. Their purpose was to protest the lack of resistance, even apparent acquiesence, of church leaders in the illegal activities of the state-run Council for Russian Orthodox Church Affairs that had orchestrated the Khrushchev persecution of Orthodoxy in the years 1959-64. The patriarch responded by banishing Eshliman and Iakunin from office, though they remained priests. More vivid, perhaps, is the example of another Moscow clergyman, Father Dimitri Dudko, who was ordained an Orthodox priest in 1960, after completing a theological education that had been interrupted by an eight and a half year prison term in a labor camp. Thus, in Dudko one sees embodied the two critical currents that assailed the patriarchate in the 1950s and 1960s. Dudko's imprisonment under Stalin, a period devoted to a life of prayer, provided the spiritual foundation for a remarkable ministry that spoke out publicly in a forthright manner to Muscovites coming to his church for spiritual counsel on matters of faith in an atheist society:

The Church never stands aside. … From this place, from which I have just greeted you on the day of Christ's Resurrection, people were exhorted to rally around and help those suffering at the front. There are other difficulties, perhaps as great as time of war pervasive sin, when vice, like rust or vermin, is corrupting our families and morally crippling the rising generation, when moral standards are disintegrating, when drunkenness, hooliganism, and murder are increasing. … [D]uring the war many were calling for help, but today for some reason they are unwilling or afraid. But the danger today is less great.

By 1972, Father Dimitri was dismissed by the patriarchate from his parish, briefly reinstated after public outcry, and then transfered to a more distant church outside Moscow. It should be noted that Father Dimitri never criticized the church leadership, but the effectiveness of his ministry and the inability of the patriarch to defend him from state authorities confirmed what many saw as the cowardice of the church leadership, as can be seen in one of his famous "question and answer" exchanges with a member of his congregation:

QUESTION: Father Dimitri, why do you set up the Church as an example? Open your eyes and look at today's clergy, even at the Patriarch himself, grovelling before the authorities, cowardly.

ANSWER: You see the inadequacies of today's clergy and point to the Patriarch himself, but are you aware that you are looking at things too superficially? Who has fewer civil rights than the Patriarch? They say he is surrounded by thousands of informers. He so much as sighs and it's heard in every government department. Everything he does against his conscience he does under pressure and, of course, out of weakness, like any man. But you don't want to be compassionate. You sit in the judge's seat and pronounce sentence.

Thus, caught between renewed persecution of a militant Communist Party seemingly bent on returning the church to its prewar status and a more energetic and determined Orthodox laity and clergy whose actions directly fed into the "democratic movement" of the 1960s and early 1970s, the Moscow patriarchate had carefully to consider its position. This was the beginning of the Pimen years, newly elected at the All-Russian National Council in May-June, 1971. Pimen has been described even by churchmen prepared to defend him as a man with "excessive fear of Soviet authorities." Under his direction, the Council shelved discussion of the 1961 statute on church affairs designed by the government to strengthen state control over parish life. Apparently the bishops found compelling the warning made by Makartsev, a deputy of the Council for Religious Affairs: "Whoever tries to resist the decrees on the parishes will get his legs broken." Moreover, the 1970s and early 1980s proved to be a period of arrests of those active in Orthodox dissent. By 1980, Solzhenitsyn was expelled from the USSR, Father Iakunin dispatched to a labor camp, Dudko, Lev Regel'son and others discredited by the KGB.

The result was a determination by the church leadership, in the words of the late Metropolitan Nikodim of Leningrad, that "the State must never again feel that it can do without the Church, as it did during the anti-religious campaign" of 1959-64. Prominent in the new policy was the effort to support fully the Soviet government's foreign policy. The patriarchate began contributing large amounts of money to the Soviet Peace Fund; Metropolitan Aleksei of Tallinn became a member of the Fund's board of directors. Financial support for the Soviet invasion of Afghanistan in 1979 and for "national liberation" struggles in Asia and Africa that are of concern to the Soviet government was now channeled through the Peace Fund. In 1977 the patriarch initiated a world conference entitled "Religious Workers for Lasting Peace, Disarmament and Just Relations among Nations." This was followed in 1982 by a second "world" conference of "Religious Workers for Saving the Sacred Gift of Life from Nuclear Catastrophe." The Soviet government has rewarded such dedication by publicly awarding Patriarch Pimen the Order of the Red Banner of Labor for his defense of peace. From the patriarch's point of view the benefit from this policy is not just recognition by the government that the church can be useful, and therefore needed, but also the added safety derived form extensive relations with churches and international organizations around the world. Unable to extend the church's role at home, the patriarchate sought support and protection from world public opinion. The price for this policy, of course, is high because it has repeatedly placed the patriarchate in a position where it must misrepresent the actual internal life of Soviet Christians. Dimitri Pospielovsky, a Canadian historian of Orthodoxy, recalls a conversation he and Metropolitan Nikodim had on this very matter:

> To my remark that it is a bad temptation for a Christian to witness a bishop not telling the truth, he retorted: 'It is you people in the West that react this way. We're used to this sort of thing in the Soviet Union, and we don't react.'
>
> 'But it is terrible,' I said, 'that lies are accepted in such a way.'
>
> 'I didn't say this was good or bad. I'm just stating a fact,' said the Metropolitan with a sad smile. And then he went on to describe his own strategy as that of a man who in dense traffic prefers to select small side roads, and thus a longer distance, while still going towards his aim, rather than get stuck in a traffic jam or end up in an accident on the main road. He hoped that in this way he would achieve more for the Church in the long run.

Nevertheless, since 1985 and the Gorbachev succession to post of General Secretary of the Communist Party of the Soviet Union, a new opportunity may have arrived for Russian Orthodoxy. Having demonstrated its international usefulness and loyalty, the church may now be invited to participate in "restructuring" *(perestroika),* particularly in areas that require a pastoral role such as in combatting alcoholism. Moreover, *perestroika* has literally meant the rebuilding and reopening of twenty-nine churches and at least one monastery. "Glasnost'" has meant the allotment of 100,000 newly printed Bibles to the Orthodox Church. Additionally, just as Gorbachev has appealed for support among Soviet intellectuals, the patriarchate now has the chance to enter into dialogue with its own previously repressed clergy and laity, many of them only recently released from prison or exile. No one should imagine that the schism between the patriarchate and church reformers will be easily resolved. In March of this year Iakunin and other dissidents urged that Pimen step down as patriarch as a first step toward reform.

It is too early to know how substantial is actually the new opportunity for reconciliation within the Orthodox church or for a larger scope for religious life within Soviet society. Legal changes are under discussion in the Council of Ministers in consultation with the Council of Religious Affairs and its "born again" bureaucratic chief Konstantin Kharchev. Perhaps there is no better way to end this talk about the nearly half-century of tension between dissent and conformity in the Russian Orthodox church than to quote a recent interview with Mr. Kharchev which suggests that a more favorable environment might be possible for Christianity, leaders and laity alike, in the USSR: "I used to treat believers in the old way. I was accustomed to thinking of them as riff-raff, backward types on a level with criminals. I had to develop a new mentality."

This is a remark in line with General Secretary Gorbachev's insistence on "new thinking." But perhaps Soviet leaders, the patriarchate, and dissenters would do better to rely on the Greek word for "rethinking," that is, "repentance," as the surest way forward on our common pilgrim path.

Part 2
Christianity and Russian Culture

The Burning Bush Mother of God [Russian, 19C.]
Benedicte Oehry Collection, Zürich, Switzerland

8

Problems of Liturgical Abuse in Sixteenth-Seventeenth Century Russia

Josef Gulka & Alexander V. Riasanovsky

University of Pennsylvania

I

In Orthodox worship, church singing is not simply choral music performed in a church to "liturgical" texts, distinguishable from secular music only by textual substance and location of performance. The very word used for worship in the Typika and Irmologia of the Slavic Churches *pesnopenie* (Old Slavonic) may be etymologized as "sung songs" or "the singing of hymns" or "songs," and indicates the intimate link between sound, word, and worship.[1] "Sacred sound," distinct from "liturgical music" and one of the "liturgical arts," is the primary medium intended to bear and express theological truth. As "sound" it has its own principles of organization and internal aesthetics. Both of these, although subordinate to the text, are organically linked to the text and must express the same aesthetic unity of a Christian Truth. Among classical Byzantine theoreticians of liturgical music,[2] the descriptive terminology and theological substructure used to discuss the relation of text to sound, and even sound to the neumatic pictograph created to represent it, are the same as that used to discuss the relation between matter and spirit in visual iconography, and their overall expression of incarnational theology. Naturally, distortions in praxis that obscure meaning or have ends other than that of revealing the text, are serious signposts of deeper problems.[3]

By the seventeenth century, the liturgical books in Russian were replete with errors and innovations which rendered the texts of the daily office almost incomprehensible. Even the archpriest Avvakum, who had led the dissent against the reforms of Patriarch Nikon (1652–1666), had recognized the need for change of some kind.[4] The problem, at least to

Avvakum, was the nature and method of *some,* but not *all,* of the Patriarch's "corrections." Nikon's reforms, however, had been imposed from the top downward through essentially extraconciliar decrees, and were based on non-Russian texts and practices. The nation had recently experienced the bitter taste of foreign intervention during the Time of Troubles, and there was considerable resentment and suspicion of anything non-Russian.[5] The rather artificial and external reforms of Nikon were doomed, if not to failure, then to controversy almost from the beginning. What was needed was a self-generated reform, structured not only on a paradigm born of the continuous historical development of the Church in Russia, but also upon the basic unified vision of Eastern Christianity.[6]

II

There were three major areas of abuse in the liturgical practices of the Russian Orthodox church of the sixteenth and seventeenth centuries:

1. *Khomoniia* (also referred to as *razdel'norechie,* or divergent speech) which concerned specific corruptions of the liturgical texts as a direct result of linguistic developments.

2. *Mnogoglasie* (not to be confused with *mnogogolosie,* or polyphonic singing) which was a problem of liturgical practice or execution.

3. *Anenaika* and *Khabuvoe Penie,* which—although beginning as issues of a purely musical nature—would result in grotesque distortions of the liturgical texts.

KHOMONIIA

The term *istinorechie,* or "true speech," is a technical term drawn from historical linguistics. It is a derivative compound of the Old Slavonic words *istina* (truth) and *rech'* (speech or tongue). It has been specifically used to describe a problem arising in the pronunciation of the liturgical texts in singing the "divine services." More specifically, the term *istinorechie* is applied when the pronunciation of the sung text corresponds to the pronunciation of the spoken vernacular. There are two historical periods during which *istinorechie* prevailed, that is to say, when the reading (chanting, singing) of the liturgical text in the hymnography was the same as common speech. The first period occurs around the eleventh and twelfth centuries, shortly after the baptism of Kievan *Rus'* (ca. 988). The second period occurs in the mid-seventeenth century, when an effort was made to bring the liturgical language employed in church singing into concord not only with everyday pronunciation, but also with seventeenth century vocabulary.[7]

When the pronunciation of a word in singing a liturgical text differs from the common spoken usage, the term *razdel'norechie,* or "divergent speech," is applied. *Razdel'norechie* is seen as a deviation from *istinorechie.* It is also a compound of two Old Slavonic words *razdeliat'* (to divide or separate) and *rech'* (speech or tongue).

Considering the crucial link between sound, text, and vernacular usage upon which Orthodoxy insists, the problem naturally assumes greater importance. The set of issues resulting from the initial deviation in pronunciation were grouped under the term *khomoniia.*[8] The origins of this term are more difficult to establish. The Soviet musicologist A. I. Rogov suggests that this term evolved from the verb form endings of the first person plural, which, if pronounced according to divergent speech practice *(razdel'norechie),* would result in the necessary root хомъ. With ъ = о, хомъ would then have been pronounced *khomo.*[9] In modern Russian, however, the letter ъ has no sound, and the ending хомъ would be pronounced *khom.* As to why, out of all the possible endings for verbs and nouns, this particular form was singled out to represent the entire problem, still remains a mystery. It may simply have been the verb ending most frequently appearing in the liturgical texts and, therefore, chosen to delineate the entire category of divergences.

An alternate hypothesis has been posited in which the term *khomoniia* is related to the Greek word ἁρμονοῖα (accord or concord). If this term were chosen in order to indicate or direct the positive resolution of the divergent factors involved, the term ἁρμονοῖα and its Slavonic equivalent хомония *(khomoniia)* would have been a simple description of the nature of the problem, as there was no accord in pronunciation.[10]

The controversy which surrounded the situation described by these terms is attested to in numerous sources from the sixteenth and seventeenth centuries.[11] Objections to *khomoniia* or *razdel'norechie* began already early in the sixteenth century, and were occasionally accompanied by isolated individual or local attempts to align the singing with the contemporary form of speech, *na rech'*. Avvakum himself writes in this regard:

> I myself sang according to the contemporary form of speech up to the time of the pestilence in Moscow.[12] A translation was made during the reign of Tsar Feodor Ivanovich, and I myself sang it many times in the Kazan' Cathedral. Since then, and to this very day, I sing in unison and according to the contemporary form of speech, for it is virtuous and according to the Scriptures ... Edicts were published during the reign of Tsar Ivan [IV] about singing in unison; and I saw *irmoi* which were written according to the contemporary form of speech, with my own eyes. These had been in the old style [in an older style of neumatic notation] at that time.[13]

Avvakum, the leader of the Old Believers, was apparently not opposed to singing in what for him was "modern" pronunciation. He recognized a real pastoral problem: a need to have the liturgy understood in the contemporary language of the people. In light of this, one can hardly accuse him of being a fanatic or obscurantist who considered any alteration in form to be a departure from the imperative to maintain the "Apostolic Faith." Avvakum sang *na rech'* because he recognized that the practice of *khomoniia* was a serious threat to the spiritual well-being of his flock. As V. Smolenskii the pre-revolutionary Russian musicologist noted in his commentary to the *Azbuka znamennogo peniia* of Alexander Mezenets, the entire issue of *khomoniia*, or radical divergence in pronunciation was already an old problem by the seventeenth century:

> The [Liturgical] texts of the fifteenth century service books already contain all the beginnings of *razdel'norechie*, or *khomoniia*, which, by the seventeenth century had developed into a problem of immense proportions. The more ancient *istinorechie* [of the eleventh and twelfth centuries] is distinguished by the continuation of the melody over the letters ь and ъ as well as by the absence of neumes over them. It is only possible for us to theorize about the pronunciation of these letters, as it had been carried over into the fifteenth century. A general examination shows, however, that the rhythmic accents in the melodies, especially the strongest of these accents, never fall on those sounds which have remained light semivowels to this day [1888]. We will go on to show that, as a consequence of the orthography involved in combining sounds, we have now altered our speech in regard to the letters ь and ъ at the end of words in modern orthography.[14]

The more ancient *istinorechie* to which Smolenskii refers (eleventh and twelfth centuries) was a period when, in speech, the letters, and were considered semi-vowels and given some form of voicing. Thus a word like дьньсь virtually unpronounceable in seventeenth century Russian [or modern Russian], could have been pronounced in common speech, and sung as *"de-ne-se"* without any difficulty. The earliest textual-musical examples, though still musically undecipherable, clearly indicate neumes, or *znamiia* placed above these semi-vowels, indicating the continuation of the melodic line over these letters.[15] There is no reason to believe that they were not pronounced.

Linguistic development is not by nature problematic, but rather often seen as an indication of cultural vitality or degeneration. In a "liturgical" culture, in which there is established a fundamental link between vernacular speech, worship, and theological truth, linguistic change becomes problematic only when the changes which occur in the language over the centuries is not reflected in the liturgical texts. Comparative studies of the melodies or melodic fragments of liturgical chant indicate that church hymnographers and singers remained basically conservative about the melodic traditions they inherited.[16]

Naturally, a linguistic shift in vowels and their subsequent voicing would necessitate some adjustment in the melodic structure of the chant which moved above these spoken sounds. Apparently reluctant to alter traditional melodies, church singers continued to voice letters (such as ь and ъ), even when such voicing was disappearing from vernacular usage. The organic change which occurred in the spoken language did not occur in the liturgical texts or in church singing.

The crucial changes in speech began to take place in parts of the southern and western territories of the Kievan hegemony during the eleventh and twelfth centuries.[17] As with most linguistic changes of this type (pronunciation, rather than syntax or grammar), the process of change took place over a long period of time and continues to be reflected in "Old" and modern Russian. The crucial linguistic changes involved two aspects: [1] the dropping of semi-vowels in most case endings and [2] the full-voicing of these semi-vowels in other specific situations.

In examining the development of full-voicing, or *polnoglasie*, as a consequent of *khomoniia*, a survey of fifteenth century liturgical texts indicates that the ensuing changes were far from automatic. The shift away from the half-voiced semi-vowels ь and ъ to the full-voiced vowel sounds e and o respectively, occur without consistency, but with increasing frequency.[18] This process must be understood as the gradual generation of an indigenous linguistic development, accompanied by the problem of regularizing corresponding orthography. Specific studies of this shift reveal that words which were previously written without the ъ (из, воз, без, for example) came to be written in the musical manuscripts with or without the final ъ even before the beginning of *razdel'norechie,* but without *znamiia* above them.[19] It is also evident that, occasionally, neuter nouns in the instrumental case (with the ending бемь) and verb forms ending in ъ, but *without* the rhythmic accent of the melody falling on them, were also written *without* the change of ъ to o. Even when light stress was placed on semi-vowels, they seem to have been replaced by full vowels. That is why it is possible to find such variants as дьньсь, деньсь, дьнесь, and дьньсь. It is also possible that the use of particular variants may have been predilected by the melodic line itself.

It must be emphasized again that the change in pronunciation was gradual. Full-voiced letters gradually began to appear in liturgical/musical texts, slowly replacing the semi-vowels. Their presence as fully voiced vowels created new problems stresses were now displaced in certain words. In manuscripts dating from the early period of *istinorechie* (eleventh and twelfth centuries) a word such as съпасъ would appear with neumes above both semi-vowels. The twelfth through the fifteenth centuries witnessed the first stage of linguistic transfer. The final ъ in съпасъ was dropped and disappears from manuscript copies. The normal stress, however, still fell upon the vowel a, and the first ъ retained its characteristic semi-vowel pronunciation. The second phase of linguistic transfer entailed the loss of vocalization in everyday speech of the first ъ. The resulting word form came to be pronounced "spas." In certain other situations, we find that the ъ was rendered as a full voiced o. The following examples are cited for comparison:[20]

12th Century Old Church Slavonic	15th Century Old Russian	17th Century Razdel'norechie
1. въньми	вънеми	вонеми
2. из горы от	из горы отъ	из горы ото
3. сълньце	сълнеце	солнеце
4. възъпии	възопии	возепии
5. израиль	израиль	израиле

As singers encountered neumes over semi-vowels, both the ь and the ъ were eventually transferred to full voicing. Thus, while the word съпасъ came to be pronounced "spas" in everyday speech, it was sung "sopaso" in the liturgical texts. Although this practice was followed in the singing of liturgical texts, it was not tolerated in the reading [chanting] of Scriptural texts, such as the appointed *paramii* (the Old Testament readings often included in festal Vespers), Gospel and epistle readings.[21] By the seventeenth century, the practice of full voicing of semi-vowels resulted in radical distortions in syllabic stress. It appears that the sixteenth and seventeenth century church musicians were either aesthetically undisturbed by the fact that the rhythmic accents of the melodic line failed to correspond to the stresses of the text or had, by that time, accepted their melodic inheritance as somehow "sanctified" and "immutable."

A parallel development should be noted. From the thirteenth to the fifteenth century, the Byzantine church, directed from Constantinople, exerted increasing pressure to eliminate both the range of theological latitude characteristic of the Golden Age of Greek patristic literature, as well as the variants in liturgical practice then still common to the differing regional communities within the Orthodox *Oekumene*. The direct relation between this move away from a healthy pluralism and the "official" schism between the Eastern and Western branches of Christianity in the eleventh century has yet to be adequately investigated. Nonetheless, this narrowing vision of Orthodoxy would naturally effect a change, or at least a growing caution, in the attitude of the hierarchy toward reform or even normal historical development within the Church. The resultant strain of legalism and literalism characteristic of much late Byzantine theology would only be compounded by the fall of Constantinople to the Turks in 1453. In this process of temporary retrenchment, the last stage of defensive reaction would be to attempt to "freeze" even the "liturgical arts" (iconography, hymnography, architecture, and so forth), increasingly cultivating a sense of "immutability" about even the more cosmetic aspects of these arts. Unity with theological truth became more a product of superficial conformity, rather than consonance with the underlying "liturgical aesthetic."

It may well have been a reflection of this general tendency which conditioned the response of Russian church musicians to the musical legacy "entrusted" to them. Their apparent "indifference" to both the divergence between vernacular usage and liturgical singing, and the distortions caused by shifts in voicing and stress, resulted in either significant changes in meaning, or even complete loss of comprehension in the liturgical texts. It is the church musicians who must ultimately bear responsibility for the widespread confusion which resulted from *khomoniia*.

What motivated these musicians—who must have understood the need for an intimate relationship between text and sound—to tolerate and even to develop and perpetuate practices which ultimately struck at the very core of the relationship, often producing chaos and confusion? While this is both an expansive and complex topic, and ultimately outside the focus of this study, a closer examination of how the shift toward full voicing was adjusted to syllabic stress while singing is directly relevant to the immediate discussion, and provides insights into the ways in which these singers hoped to preserve the chant tradition they received.

At first, full voicing was employed only where the rhythmic structure of the melodic line was left undisturbed. In other words, church musicians made a conscious effort to preserve the melody line exactly as it was received, even if the pronunciation of a given word had changed in vernacular usage (e.g., the dropping of a semi-vowel), creating a consonant cluster where none had existed before. The singers apparently persisted in retaining the vowel so that the flow of the melodic line would not be altered. Ironically, the vowel sound which the singers inserted between the consonants had little relation to the original pronunciation of ь and ъ. *Khomoniia* thus began not as degeneration or corruption, but rather as an attempt by church musicians to maintain the melodic tradition of the *znamenny* chant in its original form, regardless of the text which then underlay it.

By the seventeenth century, however, it would appear that the melodic conservatism of the singers gave way to some other motivation. In seventeenth century collections of liturgical texts, both with and without musical notation, there are frequent indications of full voicing at totally unnecessary points.[22] It appears that church musicians considered it entirely acceptable to "enhance" or "develop" the original chant line, or even the body of newly composed melodies, by the addition of an extra syllable/s or by extension through the development of key melodic motifs. It was exactly this impulse which created the confusion that prompted Tsar Aleksei Mikhailovich to create a Commission for the task of putting the body of chant material into "some kind of order." [23] Whatever reasons there might have been for ignoring the imperative for clarity of text, the results were disastrous for the liturgy. The music was astonishing in the creativity and power of the melodic lines; but no one understood the words of the prayers.

> From unnecessary full voicing and extension of the melody over unstressed vowels, it happened that either [1] a different meaning was added to the word as a result of an alphabetical configuration; [2] a different meaning of the word resulted from the modification of grammatical forms; or [3] finally absolute meaninglessness resulted.[24]

The dilemma that church musicians faced was an old one: music for its own artistic sake, or music as the medium of worship, ultimately subject to an aesthetic external to its own organization. The musician in each singer cried out to create the most beautiful chant possible; the churchman inside him was resigned to silence.

It was precisely because of this "silence" that Patriarch Iosif issued a decree in 1652, later to be confirmed by the Council of 1666–67, that all church singing must be performed *as it was spoken*.[25] It was likewise this desire for order and clarity that motivated a number of proposals to resolve the problem, among them the *Azbuka znamennogo peniia* of Alexander Mezenets (1668), offered as a musicological treatise and practical manual, but with a profound theological base and philosophical implications.

MNOGOGLASIE

The second great abuse of the age pertained to liturgical practice, and, in the sources that isolate the abuse, is often confused with the advent of harmonized music in Moscow and/or the emergence of native Russian forms of polyphony which began to appear in approximately the same period.

It was in the seventeenth century that Western-style harmonized music was first introduced into the Muscovite liturgy, and very probably under the patronage of Patriarch Nikon himself. Although Western-style liturgi-

cal music had already been adopted by the Orthodox living under the
Polish Crown, its spread into the heartland of Russia was retarded by the
conservative, anti-Western temperament of the Muscovite hierarchy with
its fear and dislike of Rome. Writing in the nineteenth century, the
musicologist A.V. Preobrazhenskii summarizes the arrival of Western-style
liturgical music into Russia as follows:

> ... It [Western-style liturgical music] gradually spread into great Russia, al-
> though it made very slow progress and was met with much anti-Western
> antagonism. This antagonism to the West reached its climax in the first years of
> the seventeenth century, when the Poles seized Moscow ... But after these
> troubles were over, the harmonized settings were gradually introduced, together
> with the staff of five lines [in contrast to the staffless neumatic or *znamenny*
> notation]. This occurred first in "Great Novgorod," and then in Moscow itself,
> until, by the beginning of the eighteenth century, nothing but the simple
> plainchant *[prostopenie]* remained in common between one monastery and
> another, every choir having its own way of harmonizing the melodies." [26]

This type of polyphonic singing was called *partesnoe penie,* or "part
singing." Confusion arose when the term *partesnoe penie* came to be
confused with two other equally descriptive terms: *mnogoglasie* and
mnogogolosie, both of which refer to the use of "many voices," but in two
very different expressions.

What is already a difficult terminological distinction is made even
more complicated by the fact that both *mnogoglasie* and *mnogogolosie* are
based on the same two roots which may be etymologized as "many"
(mnogo) and "voice" *(glas,* or *golos). Mnogogolosie* (based on the root form
golos) is a purely musical term which serves to designate a style of native
Russian polyphonic choral singing. Although *mnogogolosie* shares certain
elements in common with Western-style polyphony, its internal musical
principles are peculiar to the region and to the time period in which it
developed.[27]

Mnogoglasie (based on the root form *glas),* on the other hand, is a term
in liturgical praxis applied to an abuse which was relatively widespread in
sixteenth and seventeenth century Russia. As was the case with *khomoniia,*
complaints against *mnogoglasie* were voiced by clerics and laymen alike.
Lacking, however, the precise musical terminology of our time, the
surviving descriptions of the alleged abuses tend to be vague or confusing.
This deficiency has, in turn, generated problems of interpretation. For

example, Patriarch Germogen (1606–1612) wrote:

> We are informed that ... great disorder has occurred in church singing. According to the Holy Apostles and the laws of the Holy Fathers, one does not alter the church singing and speak in two, three, or four voices and sometimes even in five or six voices at one time. That is foreign to our Christian Law.[28]

Another such complaint was addressed to Patriarch Iosif:

> The usual royal [court] singing is insecure in many ways. It is not performed in the correct way; a second and a third is added to the initial voice, even up to five or six voices are added.[29]

At first glance, one might deduce that the issue involved was the introduction of Western-style polyphonic choral singing, based upon the use of the word "voice," a term commonly used in Western music to describe the individual musical parts in a multi-'voiced' setting. But this is not the case. Noting the phrase "a great disorder has occurred," and the verb "to speak" (говорить in the text) in the first description cited, one gets the intimation that something more is involved. The choice of the word "spoken," never customarily used in conjunction with the celebration of divine services, rather than some form of "sung" *(peti, pevati,* or *spevati),* stands out in sharp contrast. The alteration in chuch singing referred to seems to have occurred on two levels: [1] church singing is now being "spoken" and [2] more than one voice even up to five or six are being "spoken" simultaneously.

The real problem which both Patriarchs were facing was the practice of dividing the successive parts of the service being celebrated among those singers and celebrants present and, in order that the complete service be celebrated as prescribed in the Typikon, subsequently having all participants read or sing simultaneously. For example: In celebrating Vespers, Singer "A" would be appointed to chant the opening psalm (Psalm 104), "Lord I call ..." (*Gospodi vozzvakh* ...) and two *stikhera* (verses interpolated between the verses of the psalm). Singer "B" would then be given four different "Lord I call ..." *stikhera* and the next main liturgical hymn, "Gladsome Light" *(Svete Tikhiy).* Other singers present would be appointed the remaining portions of the service. Confusion naturally arose, as they were expected to sing them all *simultaneously!* The object of this practice was to make certain the service was celebrated in its entirety, without any deletions, and *po ustavu* (according to the Typikon) but in considerably less time. A five or six-hour monastic "Vigil" *(Polu-*

noshchnitsa—which generally consisted of a combined celebration of Vespers, Matins, and the First Hour, as served on the eves of feasts and every Saturday evening) could be reduced to a fraction of the time without omitting a single verse or repeated refrain. No one could be accused of altering the "tradition," since everything was done precisely as prescribed. The problem was that neither celebrants, singers, nor those attending the services could have distinguished the liturgical sequence, or possibly even heard the prayers. To compound the confusion, it appears that if more than one priest or deacon were present, even the priestly exclamations *(vozglasy)* and diaconal petitions were distributed and chanted simultaneously. Pandemonium reigned.

The eminent contemporary musicologist and composer Ivan [Johann von] Gardner suggests that the genesis of the practice of *mnogoglasie* may well have been the result of local parish churches attempting to manage a monastic *typikon*.[30] The Typikon of St. Savva, which was adopted by the Russian Church as a whole some time toward the close of the fourteenth century, is a monastic *typikon*. However suitable it may have been for monks to keep an "All-night Vigil" *(Polunoshchnitsa or Vsenoshchnoe Bdenie)*, the rigors and rhythms of the monastic order of service were not suited for parochial life, nor were they intended to be. Men with families to care for and fields to tend were not expected to spend all their time in Church. The development of the *Typikon* was essentially a monastic phenomenon, and its transferral as the "rule" for parochial life must be seen in direct relation to the "traditional" restriction of the hierarchical ranks to the monastic clergy.

Gardner points out that *mnogoglasie* was primarily a parochial problem. Monastic communities were not directly involved with the practice of this abuse, although the apparent toleration of it by some local hierarchs, whose ranks were drawn exclusively from monastic clergy, certainly implies knowledge of this practice.

ANENAIKA

The abuses which remain to be discussed are purely musical in nature and origin, and both involve the bizarre insertion of nonsense syllables at varying points within the liturgical text.

Anenaika entailed the addition of the syllables на, не, and ни, either between syllables of existing words, or to the endings or space between words of a given text. The syllables added may be related to the traditional intonational formulae which customarily preceded the text and notation of Byzantine hymns. These formulae, corresponding to intervallic relationships, served to alert the chanters to the "mode" or "tone" (*echos,* Greek) of the hymn to be sung.[31] Performance practice often allowed these formulae to be sung audibly to alert not only the chanters, but also the worshippers present who wished to participate in the singing. In the Slavonic manuscripts which contain these added syllables, insertions into the text were made, it appears, at points where the melodic line of the chant seemed to reach its musical apex.[32] A clear example of this widespread abuse can be seen in a late sixteenth century manuscript of the Magnification *(Velichanie)* from the Feast of the Annunciation (taken from the *Stikherarion,* No. 414, Collection of Trinity-Sergius Lavra, Fol. 77v and 78r.)[33] *Anenaika,* the inserted syllables *an, ne, na, a, ni* from which is derived the term itself can be observed in the third line. The figure occurs about midway in the hymn, at its melodic high point. It should be indicated, also, that if the nonsense syllables were dropped, one would be left with a rather lengthy and beautifully constructed melisma. Although a certain degree of syllabic repetition is often involved in *anenaika,* the reader should be cautioned not to construe every case of syllable repetition as *anenaika.*[34] It has been postulated that the practice of inserting these syllables entered Russian church singing in the sixteenth century via the *kondakarion* notation and style of singing, since this notational system had already formalized the intonational formulae, as well as other perfomance practice directions, into the textual and musical incipits.[35]

Another even more unusual addition to the liturgical text in musical manuscripts of the sixteenth and seventeenth centuries is the word хабува *(khabuva),* which also appears in the form of ине хабуве *(ine khabuve).* Its origins and meaning are as much a mystery today as they apparently were in the seventeenth century. Several theories have been advanced.

One such theory which appears to have been popular in the seventeenth century is mentioned in an anonymous letter to Patriarch Germogen (1606–12) on the subject of *khabuva.* Its author, obviously dissatisfied with prevailing opinions, approached certain Greeks living in Moscow at the time. They had never heard of such a thing before. It would appear to them that this occurred only in Russia.

> Some say that where хебуве is said, it means Христе Боже. Where хабува is said, it means Христа Бога; and where хабуву is said, it means Христу Богу. Still others say that it brings down the glory of God; others think that this is done for the sake of beauty. And there are still others, with whom I agree, who believe that it does not mean anything, and that only the *fita* [a particular idiomatic melodic figure] is given utterance. It appears, my Lord, that we are shaking in darkness and that no one knows the truth. ... I asked the Greeks, my Lord; Arsenii, who is Bishop of Elasson and who serves in Moscow at the Arkhangel'skii Cathedral; Ignatii, the Bishop of Skir, who was a Patriarch and knows singing very well, and is able to sing the entire *Stikherarion* [a collection usually containing the *stikhera* (verses) for the daily office in all the eight tones *(okto echoi, Gr.)*]; Ioan Damaskin, the Archimandrite of the Voskresenskii Monastery, who served in Jerusalem at the Lord's Tomb, and now lives in Moscow at the Chudov Monastery; and I also asked the scribe Feodor Kas'ianov, and this scribe knows more than one language Greek and Latin. And they said, my Lord: 'We have never heard of and do not know what you call хабува, ине, ине хабуве. We have nothing of this kind in our Greek language, in any of our books for singers or *kanonarchs*, nor is there anything like it in any other language that we know. We have never heard such a word in the singing or in the *fity*'.[36]

The author goes on to say that if these words stand for Christ God *(Khrista Boga)*, he then sees no reason why we should not sing "Christ God." He clearly considers *khabuva* to be nonsense and a distortion that should be eliminated.

Two other explanations have been advanced as to the origins of *khabuva*: [1] that it is a derivative of the Bulgarian word хабуво *(khabuvo)*, meaning "good," and [2] that it is derived from the Greek verb χαωβοω (to "open and close").[37] If the former explanation is accepted, the insertion of the particular word *khabuvo* = good was done on the same principle as the insertion of *khabuva* = Christ God: that is, the simplest, common description of God—in one case, the most basic Christological formula (Christ God); in the other, the fundamental divine attribute (goodness)—was chosen as an "appropriate" textual insertion when deemed necessary. If the second hypothesis is accepted, the selection of a functional term meaning "to open and close" could be justified only on the technical level of musical phrasing and structure, in the process of which the melodic motifs are "opened and closed" to allow for purely musical development. Both *khabuva* and *anenaika* were eliminated in the seventeenth century when the liturgical texts were again rendered *istinorechno.*

There still remains, however, the question of why these various inter- jections were introduced into the liturgical texts. The most obvious hypothesis stems from purely musical criteria. It would appear that, as melodic lines were extended or developed on purely musical bases, often a simple full voicing or vowel extension would not sufficiently support the musical line. More syllables were simply needed to accommodate specific rhythmic and melodic dimensions. These insertions were meant to facili- tate singing by providing corresponding textual support for the musical structure. Examples of these particular word additions *(khabuva)* appear in manuscripts later than the appearance of the insertions на, не, ни, etc. It may well have been that the development of some native Slavonic insertions, parallel in function to those of the Greek intonational formu- lae, may be seen as an indication of growing national identity, and possibly even of the Graecophobia increasingly evident in the Russian Church. In addition, these "new" insertions *(khabuva)* were polysyllabic and provided an even wider structural-textural base upon which church composers could build.

The issue of *khabuva* may also be related to the development of *demestvennyi* singing in Russia. *Demestvennyi* singing, related to the term *domestik (demestik, demestvennik)* used in reference to church singers in Kievan Rus', is generally regarded as a liturgical genre specifically in- tended for feasts and solemn hierarchical services.[38] The musical and textual features of *demestvennyi* singing—intricate melodic detail, consid- erable rhythmic complexity, increasingly frequent *anenaiki* and *khabuvy,* and direct notational (neumatic) links with the *kondakarion* tradition— suggest that it was probably performed by solo chanters. These solo chanters, especially if familiar with the complexities of *kondakarion* sing- ing, and the increasing tendency, especially among Byzantine and Orien- tal church singers, to ornament freely the basic chant line, may have felt equally free to ornament the melodies they were singing. The correspon- dence between the textual insertions and increased musical complexity which they supported, indicates that these insertions could possibly have

served as cue points for not only where to begin such interpretive ornamentation, but also the "style" in which the improvisation was to be
executed. As with the problems of *khomoniia* and *mnogoglasie,* the toleration of *anenaika* by church singers and hierarchy will be the subject for
examination in a future study.

The preceding survey of the distortions in the liturgical practices in
sixteenth and seventeenth century Russia reflects a period in which the
component parts of a unified system and vision had begun to dislocate. It
was a time when, among much of the laity as well as among significant
representatives of the clergy and hierarchy, there appeared to be a failure
to see in the totality of the Church's *leitourgia* an all-embracing vision of
life; a power meant to judge, inform, and transform the whole of existence; a philosophy of life shaping and challenging all ideas, attitudes, and
actions. The historical Church needed realignment with, or restoration
to, the eschatological vision of the Church. Although the very word
"restoration" implied a historical distance that contemporary observers
take for granted, the Orthodox mind, conditioned by a different vision
and a different history, perceived that phenomenon in its own light. It has
by now become a cliché of intellectual history that Orthodoxy has stressed
continuity, and that this has in turn shaped its conception and perception of passing time. It is true that Orthodoxy envisions itself as being free
of radical discontinuities from one generation to the next with the theology of the past, but it also recognizes that in the intersection of this
tradition with the immediate historical moment, misalignments can and
do appear. Orthodox ecclesiology, in fact, demands the ability of the
Church to correct itself. It must not be defined in terms of an unreconstructed past. The Orthodox mind, then—in its very identity and structures of thought—presumes that the past will not only reveal itself, but
will also integrate and unite the present. Within this conception, each
Christian generation functions as a link in a historical chain, moving
linearly as it passes through time.

The seventeenth and eighteenth centuries would produce a variety of
re-evaluations, responses, and proposed restorations and restructurings of
this vision. Although prompted by the increase in liturgical abuses, the
range and scope of these restorations went far beyond the immediacies of
liturgical practice. Corruptions of the liturgical texts of the sort docu-

mented in this study could not be tolerated in Orthodox worship. Clarity of vision and text is central to that "reasonable worship" to which Orthodox Christians are called.

It was, in fact, the same problem which confronted Kyril and Methodios when faced with transmitting and adapting the superbly defined liturgies of Byzantine Christianity, replete with their supportive aesthetic, to the native tongue of the Bulgars. History indicates that they were willing to sacrifice certain aesthetic refinements in order to uphold the central vision of the unity of theology, liturgy, and the Christian life. Vladimir's acceptance of Christianity and the Baptism of the *Rus'* presented a similar challenge. It is not intransigence, obscurantism, and ossification that characterizes the history of Orthodox Christianity among the Slavs, especially in Russia, but rather the ability, if not the mandate, to adapt to the needs, requirements, and even the often resultant distortions generated among the faithful in each moment of history. The celebration of a millenium of Orthodox Christianity in Russia attests to its vitality, and to its ability to preserve an essential vision in a consistent process of adaptation; a process consistent with the principle of "legacy" as a vehicle not only for meaning, but for change.

NOTES

1. In Byzantine liturgical texts, the verb *proskinisein* etymologized as "to fall down, or bow down" is customarily used to describe the act of worshiping. (e.g. *Deute proskinisomen* = "Come, Let us worship.") The singing of liturgical hymns or services was called *'imnodia.* In the Slavic Churches, however, the terminology developed a different focus. While retaining an equivalent verb for "the act of worshiping" *poklonit'* (e.g. *Priidite poklonimsya* = "Come, Let us worship."), the word used to describe the singing of liturgical services *pesnopenie* (which may be etymologized as 'sung songs,' or the 'singing of songs') soon supplanted the former as the standard term to describe the act of worshiping. The Stoglav Council of the Russian Church (1551) decreed that "... [the faithful] should come to the holy churches ... and with faith and love should stand for all "divine services" *(pesnopenie).* [*Stoglav: Deianiia sobora 1551.* general editor, S. A. Belokurov (Moscow, 1890), Ch. 38; p. 160-62.] In the *Tipikon* (Sl. *ustav,* which refers to that manual which specifies how elements from the various hymnographic cycles—annual, festal, weekly, etc.—are to be combined for a specific service), all public worship services were designated as *pesnopenie:* "It must be known that, as we have said earlier about singing, according to the tradition there is to be no other ordo in the cenobitic life than the one which

requires the singing of particular psalms or some other service." [*Tipikon* (Moscow: Sinodal'naia tipografiia, 1906), Ch. 37, p. 454].

2. A line of patristic writers from Basil the Great, John Chrysostom, Maximos the Confessor, John of Damascus, Theodore the Studite, Germanos of Constantinople, and Simeon of Thessalonike among others have used a common descriptive and theological framework, i.e. "sacramental," when discussing the nature of the liturgy and its concomitant liturgical media (icons, hymnography, architecture, etc.). More specifically, the musicians and hymnographers themselves—John of Damascus, Theodore the Studite, John Koukouzeles, and others—have adopted this framework and describe their art in specifically incarnational terminolgy. For a discussion of the Byzantine notational systems, especially neumatic and systemic symbolism, see: R. Verdeil, *La musique byzantine* (Paris, 1962), Chaps. V, VI, VII, and H. J. W. Tillyard, *The Hymns of the Sticherarium for November* (Copenhagen, 1936).

3. Regarding the importance of the liturgy in Orthodox worship, see Appendix 1.

4. *Zhitie protopopa Avvakuma im samim napisannoe i drugie ego sochineniia,* ed. N. K. Gudzy, V. M. Malyshev, *et al.* (Moscow, 1960), pp. 105ff.

5. Sergei Platonov, *The Time of Troubles: A Historical Study of the Internal Crisis and Social Struggle in 16th and 17th Century Muscovy* (Lawrence: U. of Kansas Press, 1970), pp. 150-60.

6. At approximately the same times as the liturgical abuses were being isolated and attempts to correct them began, concomitant problems in the realm of Church administration arose. In this connection see Appendix 2.

7. A. I. Rogov, *Muzykal'naia estetika Rossii XI–XVIII vekov* (Moscow, 1973), pp. 37-39.

8. A. V. Preobrazhenskii, *Kul'tovaia muzyka v Rossii* (Leningrad: Academia, 1924), p. 46-48.

9. Rogov, *Muzykal'naia estetika,* p. 12.

10. A. V. Preobrazhenskii, *Ocherk istorii tserkovnago peniia v Rossii* (Petrograd, 1915), p. 63.

11. Rogov, *Muzykal'naia estetika,* pp. 58–93.

12. The reference is to the plague of 1654-55, which the musical theoretician Alexander Mezenets mentions in relation to the dissolution of the first commission established to reform the existent texts. For a discussion of the developments leading up to the formation of this commission, see S. V. Smolenskii, *Azbuka znamennogo peniia: izveshchenie o soglasneishikh pometak startsa Aleksandra Meznetsa (1668)* [Kazan', 1888], p. 38 and ff.

13. *Zhitie protopopa Avvakuma,* p. 91. A "Kanon" is a highly complex multi-sectioned liturgical poem, composed of nine sections, or Odes. Each Ode is thematically related to one of nine appointed Scriptural "Canticles" detailing specific typological images or characters from the Old Testament. Each Ode is initiated with an *Irmos,* which is strictly metered and sets the metrical model for

the successive *troparia* or verses (usually fourteen in number) which follow the *irmos.*

14. Smolenskii, *Azbuka,* p. 34. The word actually used by Mezenets can be translated as "stress." When referring to textual components, we have retained the usage of "stress"; and, when referring to the musical components of a melodic line, we have used the word "accent."

15. Metallov, *Bogosluzhebnoe,* p. 115.

16. For a discussion of this topic, see: Milos Velimirovic, *Byzantine Elements in Early Slavic Chant* (Copenhagen, 1960).

17. Ivan Gardner, *Bogosluzhebnoe penie Russkoi Pravoslavnoi Tserkvi: Sistema, sushchnost'. istoriia* (Jordanville, NY: Holy Trinity Monastery, 1980-82), Vol. 1, pp. 306-08.

18. S. V. Smolenskii, "O drevnerusskikh pevcheskikh notatsiiakh," *Pamiatniki drevnei pis'mennosti i iskusstva.* CXLV (St. Petersburg, 1901), p. 111 and ff.

19. *Ibid.,* p. 115.

20. Smolenskii, *Azbuka,* p. 36.

21. Gardner, *Bogosluzhebnoe,* p. 404. See also Smolenskii, *Azbuka,* p. 35.

22. N. D. Uspenskii, *Drevnerusskoe pevcheskoe iskusstvo,* 2nd ed. (Moscow: Sovetskii kompozitor, 1971), p. 64.

23. Smolenskii, *Azbuka,* Introduction. See also Platonov, *Time of Troubles,* Section III.

24. N. D. Uspenskii, *Obraztsy drevnerusskogo pevcheskogo iskusstva* (Leningrad: Muzyka, 1971), p. 106.

25. V. M. Metallov, "K voprosu o komissiakh po ispravleniiu bogosluzhebnykh pevcheskikh knig russkoi tserkvi v XVII veke," *Bogoslovskii vestnik* (May 1912), p. 99. See also Smolenskii, *Azbuka,* for a general discussion of the intended results from Mezenets's proposals.

26. A. V. Preobrazhenskii, *Ocherk istorii tserkovnago peniie v Rossii* (Petrograd, 1915), p. 126.

27. For a discussion of the internal principles of indigenous Russian polyphony, see Maksim Brazhnikov, *Litsa i fity znamennogo raspeva* (Leningrad: Muzyka, 1984). See also W. J. Birkbeck, "Some Notes upon Russian Ecclesiastical Music, Ancient and Modern." *Proceedings of the Musical Association,* XVII (London, 1890-91), p. 140 and following.

28. As cited in Metallov, "K voprosu," p. 129.

29. *Ibid.,* p. 130.

30. Gardner, *Bogosluzhebnoe,* Vol. 1, p. 447.

31. For a discussion of "tone" *(echos)* in Orthodox liturgical music, see Appendix 3.

32. his example is cited in Gardner, *Bogosluzhebnoe,* p. 450.

33. For a reproduction and discussion of the example cited, see Appendix 4.

34. As church composers began to explore the musical elements of Slavic chant and to develop their own internal musical structure, the "symphonic" construction of the melodic motifs came to be emphasized. The result was a continuing expansion of the original motif through repetition, ornamentation and variation. To support this development, certain syllables, expecially in key words or refrain texts, were repeated to supply a base for the melodic architecture.

35. See Egon Wellesz, *A History of Byzantine Music and Hymnography* (Cambridge: Cambridge University Press, 1971).

36. As cited in Rogov, *Muzykal'naia estetika,* pp. 59-65. Although the Greek hierarchs cited in this quote were not aware of any phenomenon comparable to *khabuva* "in any language we know," or had "never heard such a word in singing," Bulgarian and Serbian musical manuscripts from an even earlier period (fifteenth century for Serbian, fifteenth and possibly even fourteenth century for the Bulgarian sources), contain clear examples of both *anenaika* and *khabuva,* the use of which seem to follow the same principles as the later examples from Russian sources. For a good introduction to Medieval Serbian chant, see *Stara Srpska Muzika: Primeri tserkvenikh pesama iz XV veka,* edited by Stana Djuric-Klajn; prepared by Dimitrije Stefanovic. Institute of Musicology, Serbian Academy of Sciences and Arts. Monograph series, Vol. 15/1, Belgrade, 1975. See especially pp. 1–51 and 157–89.

37. Rogov, *Muzykal'naia estetika,* p. 65.

38. For a discussion of the development and characteristics of *demestvennyi* singing and notation, see Ivan Gardner, *Das Problem des altrussischen demestischen Kirchengesangs und seiner linienlosen Notation* (Munich, 1964).

39. The *Epanagogue,* a ninth century Byzantine law code, is generally believed to have been written by the celebrated Patriarch Photios, Patriarch of Constantinople (858-867 and 878-886), during his second seating upon the Patriarchal throne. It is generally considered the first such code to detail the relations between the state and the Church, particularly as far as the respective duties and prerogatives of the Emperor and Patriarch were concerned. It has been conclusively shown that the *Epanagogue* was officially proclaimed law, and had been repeatedly used as such in the Byzantine Empire, in Russia, and in other parts of the Byzantine hegemony. It is likewise considered one of the bases of Russian Canon Law. For a discussion of the place of the *Epanagogue* in Russian Canon Law, see: Leopold Karl Goetz, *Kirchenrechliche und kulturgeschichtliche Denkmaler Altrusslands nebst Geschichte des russischen Kirchenrechts* (Stuttgart: Verlag von Ferdinand Enke, 1905), pp. 1–62.

BIBLIOGRAPHY

Beckwith, R. Sterling. *Alexander Dmitrievich Kastal'skii (1856-1926) and the Search for a Native Russian Choral Style.* Ph.D. dissertation. Cornell University, 1969.

Beliaev, Viktor. *Drevnerusskaia muzykal'naia pis'mennost'.* Moscow: Gosudarst-vennoe muzykal'noe izdatel'stvo, 1962.

_____. "Rannee russkoe mnogogolosie." *Studia Memoriae Belae Bartok Sacra.* Budapest: Academia, 1956.

Birkbeck, W. J. "Some Notes upon Russian Ecclesiastical Music, Ancient and Modern." *Proceedings of the Musical Association,* XVII. London, 1890-91.

Brazhnikov, Maksim V. *Drevnerusskaia teoriia muzyki.* Leningrad: Muzyka, 1972.

_____. *Litsa i fity znamennogo raspeva.* Leningrad: Muzyka, 1984.

_____. *Novye pamiatniki znamennogo rospeva.* Leningrad: Muzyka, 1967.

_____. *Pamiatniki znamennogo rospeva.* Leningrad: Muzyka, 1974.

_____. *Puti razvitiia i zadachi rasshifrovki znamennogo rospeva 12-18 vv.* Moscow-Leningrad, 1949.

Buketoff, Igor. "Russian Chant" in *Music in the Middle Ages.* New York, 1940.

Djuric-Klajn, Stana, editor. *Stara Srpska Muzika: primeri tserkvenikh pesama iz xv veka.* Prepared by Dmitrije Stefanovic. Institute of Musicology. Serbian Academy of Sciences and Arts. Monograph series, Vol. 15/I.

Findeizen, Nikolai. *Ocherki po istorii muzyki v Rossii.* 2 vols. Moscow-Leningrad: Gosudarstvennoe muzykal'noe izdatel'stvo, 1928.

Gardner, Ivan [Johann von] *Bogosluzhebnoe penie Russkoi Pravoslavnoi Tserkvi: Sistema, sushchnost', istoriia.* 2 volumes. Jordanville, NY: Holy Trinity Monastery, 1980–82.

_____. *Ein Handgeschriebenes Lehrbuch der alt- russischen Neumschrift.* Bayerische Akademie der Wissenschaften. Heft 57. Munich, 1963–72.

_____. *Das Problem des altrussischen demestischen Kirchengesangs und seiner linienlosen Notation.* Munich, 1964.

Goetz, Karl Leopold. *Kirchenrechtliche und kulturgeschichtliche Denkmaler Al-trusslands nebst Geschichte des russischen Kirchenrechts.* Stuttgart: Verlag von Ferdi-nand Enke, 1905.

Hoeg, Karsten. "The Oldest Slavonic Tradition of Byzantine Music." *Proceedings of the British Academy,* XXXIV. London, 1953-54.

Lisitsyn, Mikhail. *Pervonachal'nyi slaviano-russkii tipikon.* Saint Petersburg, 1911.

Metallov, Vasily M. *Bogosluzhebnoe penie russkoi tserkvi v period domongol'skii.* Moscow, 1912.

_____. *Russkaia simiografiia.* Moscow, 1912.

_____. "K voprosu o komissiakh po ispravleniiu bogosluzhebnykh pevcheskikh knig russkoi tserkvi v XVII veke." *Bogoslovskii vestnik.* May 1912.

Morosan, Vladimir. "Penie and Musikiia: Aesthetic Changes in Russian Liturgi-cal Singing During the Seventeenth Century." *St. Vladimir's Theological Quarterly.* 23 (1979) New York, 149–79.

Platonov, Sergei F. *The Time of Troubles: A Historical Study of the Internal Crisis and Social Struggle in 16th and 17th Century Muscovy.* Lawrence: University of Kansas Press, 1970.

Preobrazhenskii, Antonin Viktorovich. *Kul'tovaia muzyka v Rossii.* Leningrad: Academia, 1924.

_____. *Muzykal'nyi slovar'.* Entries in the *Musical Dictionary* of Hugo Reiman. Moscow: Jurgenson, 1901-04.

_____. *Ocherk istorii tserkovnago peniia v Rossii.* Petrograd, 1915.

Razumovskii, Dmitri. *Bogosluzhebnoe penie pravoslavnoi Greko-Rossiiskoi Tserkvi.* Vol I: *Teoriia i praktika tserkovnogo peniia.* Moscow, 1886.

_____. *Tserkovnoe penie v Rossii.* 3 vols. Moscow, 1867-69.

Rogov, A. I., editor. *Muzykal'naia estetika Rossii XI-XVII vekov.* Moscow: Muzyka, 1973.

Skrebkov, Sergei. *Russkaia khorovaia muzyka XVII-nachala XVIII veka.* Moscow: Muzyka, 1973.

Smolenskii, Stepan V. *Azbuka znamennogo peniia: izveshchenie o soglasneishikh pometakh startsa Aleksandra Meznetsa (1668).* Kazan', 1888.

_____. "O drevnerusskikh pevcheskikh notatsiiakh." *Pamiatniki drevnei pis'mennosti i iskusstva.* CXLV. St. Petersburg, 1901.

Stoglav: Deianiia sobora 1551. General editor, S.A. Belokurov. Moscow, 1890.

Swan, Alfred J. "Harmonizations of the Old Russian Chants." *Journal of the American Musicological Society.* Summer 1949.

_____. *Russian Music and its Sources in Chant and Folksong.* New York: W.W. Norton and Co., 1973.

Tcherepnin, Alexander. *Anthology of Russian Music.* Bonn, 1966.

Tipikon. Moscow: Sinodal'naia tipografia, 1906.

Uspenskii, Nikolai. *Drevnerusskoe pevcheskoe iskusstvo.* 2nd edition. Moscow: Sovetskii kompozitor, 1971.

_____. *Obraztsy drevnerusskogo pevcheskogo iskusstva.* Leningrad, 1971.

_____. "Problema metodologii obucheniia ispolnitel'skomu masterstvu v drevnerusskom pevcheskom iskusstve." *Musica antiqua Europae orientalis. Acta scientifica* (Bydgoscz: Academia, 1967), 467-501.

Velimirovic, Milos. *Byzantine Elements in Early Slavic Chant.* Copenhagen, 1960.

Verdeil, R. *La Musique byzantine.* Paris, 1962.

Wellesz, Egon. *A History of Byzantine Music and Hymnography.* 2nd edition. Oxford: Cambridge University Press, 1962.

Zhitie protopopa Avvakuma im samim napisannoe i drugie ego sochineniia. Edited by N. K. Gudzy, V.M. Malyshev, *et al.* Moscow, 1960.

APPENDIX

1. To those unfamiliar with Byzantine Christianity's understanding of the relation between theology and liturgy, liturgical reform as a point of entry and primary insight to the problems of the Russian Church during this period (fifteenth-seventeenth centuries) may seem like undertaking major structural re-evaluations by observing ornamental decoration, often reduced at best to cultic, and at worst to cosmetic distinction. This approach would serve only to further fragment the basic unity of a common experience and vision fundamental to Orthodoxy, and ultimately mislead the observer of subsequent realignments. The purpose of theology as a discipline, according to the Orthodox view, is the orderly and consistent presentation, explication, and defense of the Church's faith. This "faith" is both theology's "source" and its "object." Change, whatever its nature, must occur within the guidelines developed from the theological ground-base. The entire structure and method of theology depend, therefore, on how one understands the nature of its relationship to that "source," that is, to the faith of the Church.

It was in the West, at first, that the source of theology began to be identified with a specific number of textually bound "data"—Scriptural, patristic, Conciliar—which as *loci theologici* were to supply speculation with its subject matter and criteria. Hence, the increasing rejection from the theological process of any direct relation to, or dependence upon experience. Yet, it is precisely faith as experience, total and living, that constitutes the source and context of theology for Eastern Christians. It is seen as a search for words and concepts adequate to, and expressive of, the continuing experiences of the Church; a search for "reality," not "propositions." It must be a "reality" in which theological pluralism is perfectly compatible with fundamental unity. For Eastern Christians, "faith" is not mere assent to doctrine, but living relations with certain, specific historical events.

The relation of liturgy to theology is likewise not to be found simply in cultic semiotics. Drawing upon a well developed pre-Christian usage, the early Christian communities applied the term *leitourgia* to those actions, ministries, and offices within the Church community through which the "Church" manifested and fulfilled her nature and vocation. Among the many *leitourgia,* the communal worship of God the "Divine Liturgy" *(Agia leitourgia)* was regarded as where most precisely the place and function of all creation was revealed. Its understanding and connotations were not cultic, but cosmical, ecclesiological, and eschatological. It was not a mere synonym for "rites," or cultic worship. In Orthodox theology, from the very beginning, the "Divine Liturgy" was seen as the point where the Church, as the "New Creation," informed not only the world, but herself of her calling. It was understood as both vessel and content. To reduce the "Divine Liturgy" to cultic categories and its definition to a "sacred act of worship," set apart as such not only from the "profane" areas of life, but even from all other activities in the church itself, is, from the Orthodox perspective, fundamentally and falsely to deprive it of its prophetic and epiphanic nature.

In a liturgical culture, "Truth," as it is understood, has an aesthetic. It is the purpose of that aesthetic not only to represent that "Truth," but also to provide a key, a point of entry into the reality of that "Truth." Its dynamic is that of true metaphor not in the conventional modern usage as a set of images that "stand for" something else, but rather a means by which the limitations of our perceptions are lifted, and we are borne to a new level of experience and comprehension. This aesthetic must resound in all dimensions of life, both private and communal: from political ideology to household economics, from philosophic speculation to private and public worship. Distortions in liturgy, especially on the issues of consonance with the aesthetic base, ultimately reflect cosmic and eschatological misperceptions. In the Orthodox vision, if the liturgy grows obscure, either from cultic legalism, nominalism, or minimalism, from linguistic or aesthetic inconsistencies, it ceases to be what it *should*, and more importantly, what it *must* be. Compounded by the ever present tendency to separate visibly, and thus to dislocate "Ortho-doxy" from "Ortho-praxis," the examination of liturgical abuses often provides the key source of dislocation, and ultimately the strategy for realignment.

2. By the sixteenth and seventeenth centuries, a second area badly in need of reform was the administrative structure which had developed to reinforce the unity of all the concomitant dynamics of "Liturgy." Although beyond the scope of this paper, a brief note needs to be made. While the often alleged total independence of each local community during the first two centuries is nothing more than a myth, the fathers of the First Nicene Council (325 A.D.), on the other hand, did *not* try to establish geographical, administrative mega-structures. [For a discussion of this topic see: Pierre L'Huillier (Bishop Peter), "Ecclesiology in the Canons of the First Nicene Council," *St. Vladimir's Theological Quarterly.* Vol. 27, No. 2 (1983)] The Canons of Nicea I contain no definition of any jurisdictional power beyond that given to Metropolitan Bishops (Bishops of large or important cities). They neither tried to establish, nor even envisioned a supra-Metropolatinal system. It is from these essential canonical foundations through what would become the chief source of Byzantine (and later Russian, specifically Nikonian) theories of Church-state relations, the ninth century *Epanagogue*[39] of the celebrated Patriarch Photios itself used to define the respective duties and privileges of Emperor and Patiarch that an unraveling of the development of supra-Metropolatinal (i.e. Patriarchal), regional primacies needs to be undertaken.

3. There is a single system which governs the musical style and organization of the performance of liturgical singing for all the branches of the Orthodox Church. This system, which is common not only to Eastern Orthodox churches, but also to Roman and certain other non-Orthodox churches, is based upon a set of eight musical "modes" or "tones" (Greek: *echos;* Sl.: *glas;* Latin: *tonus).* The system as a whole is called the *Oktoechos* in Greek, the *Osmoglasie,* in Slavonic. Each "tone" functions as a complete musical language, consisting of a set of intervallic relationships, melodic fragments, and pitch centers toward which cadential figures gravitate. This set of eight musical "languages" is paralleled by eight sets of prayers and hymn texts for the changeable sections of the daily office. Each set of prayers and hymns

covers a weekly liturgical cycle. Beginning with the Sunday after Pascha (Easter), and for the entire week that follows, the prayers, hymns, and melodies of Tone I are sung. The second Sunday after Pascha moves to Tone 2, etc., through the entire eight-week cycle, at which time the cycle is repeated. Most liturgical hymns, whether found musically notated, or by simple text citation, are supplied with a designation of the tone in which the hymn is to be performed. When the liturgical books were translated from Greek to Old Slavonic, these designations of the "tone" were retained.

4. *The Magnification of the Annunciation (Velichanie)*

1.] Ар ха гге ле ́скы и гла со

2.] во ни е мо ти чи ста я

3.] о ле та ни__ [аи не не на а ни]

4.] ра доу и ся об ра до ван на я

5.] го спо де с то бо ю

This example is taken from a *Stikherarion* (No. 414, of the Library of Trinity-Sergius Lavra, Fol. 77v and 78r.) This particular hymn is taken from the Matins service celebrated for the Feast of the Annunciation. It is sung while, in a solemn procession of clergy and servers, the icon of the Feast is carried to the center of the church and placed on a *tetrapod* (special stand used for the holding of icons to be venerated). *Anenaika* (the inserted syllables *an, ne, na, a, ni*) can be observed in the third line within the brackets. At this point the musical line not only reaches its apex, but also becomes more elaborate or ornamented. The reader who is familiar with Russian hymnographic texts in Slavonic, might also notice the presence of the effects of full voicing of semi-vowels in the following places — line 1: гласо *(glaso)*, line 2: вопиемо *(vopiemo)*, and line 5: Господе *(Gospode)*.

9

The Transformation of the Russian Sanctuary Barrier and the Role of Theophanes the Greek

Maria Cheremeteff

California College of Arts and Crafts

The iconostasis in its classic form as found in the Russian Orthodox churches in the beginning of the fifteenth century and what is now the standard of the Orthodox church, is a high screen (Figure 1) completely obscuring the sanctuary and the activity of the priest from view of the congregation in the nave.[1] It functions as an architectural picture frame for the insertion of permanently fixed panel icons. These, set out in rows, reveal the divine dispensation. In the topmost row are the patriarchs with the prophets below them. Underneath the prophets are the festival icons and below these is the great *Deesis,* where the Virgin Mary and Saint John the Baptist accompanied by the archangels Michael and Gabriel, Apostles, Church Fathers, and other Saints turn toward Christ the Judge to intercede for mankind. On the royal doors are represented the Annunciation and the four Evangelists. On either side in the Local row are two icons, usually of the Pantocrator and of the Virgin and Child along with an icon of a local saint or a liturgical feast to which the church is dedicated. A number of variants are possible according to the elaborateness of the iconostasis and local custom.

The iconostasis is one of the most distinctive features of an Eastern Orthodox church, and throughout its long development it became an important architectural feature of the interior of the church. But the opaque barrier was not always part of the liturgical furnishings of the East Christian churches.[2] It developed on its own and was not a result of a ruling or an establishment of an ecclesiastical authority.[3] This complicated any attempt to follow the evolution from the open to the closed opaque sanctuary barrier. A dilemma results in an attempt to ascribe a precise date for the actual time and place when the open sanctuary barrier was transformed into a grandiose architectural picture frame for the insertion of panel icons.

Since antiquity waist-high barriers, templons, set off the Roman Emperor from the crowd on public occasions. A representation of one such barrier may be seen on a bas relief on the base of the fourth-century obelisk of Theodosius (379–395), which still stands in the middle of the Hippodrome at Constantinople (Figure 2). A reference to a similar type of barrier may be found in a fourth century Panegyric on the building of churches by Eusebius, which is one of the earliest sources to mention an altar barrier.[4]

The original templon, an open barrier, consisted of individual parapet slabs separated by colonnettes equal to them in height. This waist-high screen separating the sanctuary from the nave is found in the earliest basilicas. By the end of the fifth century it developed into a taller partition. The vertical posts sprouted colonnettes or were replaced by columns upon which was laid an entablature. A change first occurred in the sixth century in the Hagia Sophia in Constantinople with a vertical extension of twelve colonnettes which exceeded the height of the slabs and created an upper colonnade.[5] Soon after, an architrave was placed on top of extended colonnettes to ensure greater stability to the structure and was referred to in ecclesiastical literature by the name of *kosmitis*.[6] The ensuing development of the sanctuary barrier allowed the arrangement of icons atop the *kosmitis,* including images of the cross, Christ, and the local saint.[7] The epistyle of the open screen of the crypt of St. Artemios in the church of St. John the Baptist in Oxeia (Figure 3) has been reconstructed by Mango to have consisted of a representation of Christ, John the Baptist, and St. Artemios.[8] Later, other icons were added to these until the entire architrave was completely filled with icons.

With the triumph of Orthodoxy in 843, which reinstated icon veneration following its ban and a systematic destruction of icons during the Iconoclast Period (721–843), both the liturgy and the system of church decoration began to be formulated. The only change at that time in the sanctuary barrier was a continued addition of painted icons to the epistyle. The Middle Byzantine (843–1204) sanctuary barrier was a relatively open screen of three or more bays closed by low parapet slabs and divided by colonnettes supporting a decorated epistyle. This is confimed by evidence from the Byzantine provinces as well as Constantinopolitan remains. Sections of the Typikon, or foundation charter, concerning the censing and lighting of the Pantocrator church (Zeyrek Camii) in the Pantocrator Monastery in Constantinople[9] provides convincing evidence upon which fragments, both literary and archaeological, of other barriers in Constantinople might cautiously be reassembled. Megaw[10] and Epstein[11] have reconstructed a templon screen of four colonnettes joined at their base by marble slabs and supporting an epistyle decorated with a series of images (Figure 4). However, their reconstruction of the screen is not a twelfth-century form, but, rather, a later reconstructed form after the Latin occupation (1204–1261).[12]

The *proskynetaria* is a venerated image from the Greek *proskynesis* (veneration). The *proskynetaria* are icons in that they are true devotional images of either Christ, the Virgin Mary, or a local saint of the church which appear, except in cases of limited space, on the piers flanking the sanctuary barrier, or are portable icons placed on either side of the central portal *(aiyae therae).*[13] Evidence from the best examples of Middle Byzantine monuments demonstrates that the *proskynetaria* images, which later will appear within the intercolumniations of the local row, have not yet left their traditional places in these churches on adjacent walls of the apse and the eastern pillars.

The *proskynetaria* image had not yet been transposed from their traditional places on the Western face of the Eastern pillars of the bema to the intercolumniation spaces of the local row in St. Sophia in Ohrid,[14] St Panteleimon in Nerezi[15] (Figures 5 and 6), and in the Katholikon of Daphni near Athens[16] (Figure 7). Not only the Middle Byzantine monuments, but also monuments dating to the thirteenth and fourteenth centuries, provide evidence that icons still kept their place on the eastern piers. Kalenderhane Camii,[17] which no longer has its barrier, retains fragments of the icon frames. St. Mary Pammakaristos (Fetiye Camii),[18] dated to 1300 (Figure 8) at St. Savior in the Chora (Kariye Camii)[19] in the early fourteenth century (Figure 9), retains mosaic *proskynesis* icons on the west face of the pier south of the bema.

Middle and Later Byzantine sanctuary barriers, then, did not exceed two or three rows of icons, and did not include the *proskynetaria* image within the intercolumniation of the local row.[20] In such form the barrier reached Russia. Its size was clearly reflected both in literary accounts and manuscript illuminations. It was described in Greek sources as a *thoraxis*, in Russian *nagrudnik* (to the level of the chest) or *pogrudnik* (up to the chest).[21] According to Russian primary literary sources, the sanctuary barrier was referred to as *peregrada* (partition), *zagrada* (barrier), derived from the word *zagorodit'* (to block), and *ograda* (fence), derived from the word *ogradit'* (to protect), In the Troitsa-Sergieva Lavra typicon, the height of the iconostasis is mentioned in the description of the entrance of the brethren into the nave of the church, following the completion of a compline, *polunochnitsa*, sung in the narthex. Upon reaching the sanctuary barrier, they performed *proskynesis* (prostration) three times before the royal doors of the sanctuary, venerating the cross surmounting the altar screen door.[22] The accessibility of the cross for veneration suggests a low screen. Another example of an open sanctuary barrier before which Christ is seen distributing the Communion to his Apostles is represented in the mosaic of *Christ Giving Communion to the Apostles* in the church of St. Michael of Kiev (Figure 10). These mosaics date from 1111–1112.

In Russia the iconostasis was transformed into a solid screen when spaces between the parapet slabs and the epistyle were filled between the columns with devotional panel icons, when individual panel icons were added to the epistyle, when the size of the individual icons on the epistyle was increased, and when additional rows of panel icons were added to the architrave. The innovative step toward this transformation was realized by Theophanes the Greek and his assistants, Prokhor of Gorodets and Andrei Rublev, in the Annunciation Cathedral in the Moscow Kremlin in 1405 and became the point of departure for all subsequent development of the iconostasis (Figures 11 and 12.) It was here that he transformed the sanctuary barrier into a grandiose architectural picture frame for the insertion of permanently fixed panel icons. This created a completely closed wall behind which the major part of the liturgy is performed. By enlarging the dimensions of individual panels, introducing full-length Deesis figures, and adding perhaps the Prophets Row on the epistyle, he contributed towards a vertical expansion of the iconostasis. The lateral expansion was brought about through an increased flexibility in the selection and scale of the Deesis Row icons.

A letter written about 1415 by Epifanii the Wise *(Premudryi)* to Kiril of Tver'[23] provides essential biographical information concerning the life and career of Theophanes the Greek and also offers a glimpse into his deeply philosophical nature and creative genius. It is clear from the letter that Theophanes was as skilled an icon painter as he was a miniaturist and a monumental painter. His career is traced by his friend Epifanii in chronological order from the capital of Byzantium to Galata (Genoese quarter of Constantinople), to Chalcedon (on the opposite side of the Bosporus), to the colony of Kaffa (now Theodosia in the Crimea), to Novgorod, to Nizhnii Novgorod, and finally to Moscow. The letter, together with the Trinity *(Troitskaia)* and Novgorod *(Novgorodskaia)* Chronicles *(Letopis')*, identify the monuments completed in the Russian cities. The Novgorod Chronicle[24] makes an entry under 1378 (6886) as the year of his visit to Novgorod where he worked on the Transfiguration Church *(Spas Preobrazhenie)* on Il'ina Street. The Epifanii letter and the Trinity Chronicle[25] give a full account of his work in Moscow and mention the Cathedral of Archangel Michael *(Sviatogo Mikhaila)* of 1399 (6907) and the Cathedral of the Annunciation *(Sviatogo Blagoveshcheniia)* of 1405 (6913). Although neither of the two sources specifically state that the iconostasis is the work of Theophanes the Greek, Prokhor of Gorodets, and Andrei Rublev, Grabar[26] has rightly pointed out that the iconostasis formed a major part of the decorative ensemble and was, therefore, painted by leading artists. The earlier cathedral was torn down to make room for a new one built in 1484 for Ivan III. The icons from the iconostasis were removed to the new cathedral.[27]

With the enlargement of the individual panels of the Deesis Row, Theophanes set a precedent for the subsequent transformation that led to a new type of iconostasis with five or even six tiers, and permanently fixed icons within the local row. Increase in the dimensions of individual panels of the iconostasis contributed toward its vertical expansion. Each panel of the Deesis Row in the Annunciation Cathedral measures six by three feet. By 1408 the individual panels of the Deesis Row by Andrei Rublev and Daniil Cheryi from the Dormition Cathedral in Vladimir reached an unprecedented height of 10 feet 3.5 inches (3.14 meters) and also included the Prophets Row.[28]

The size of both the Byzantine and early Russian panels was considerably smaller than the size of early fifteenth-century Russian panels which consisted predominantly of half figures.[29] At the end of the fourteenth century the half-length Deesis was very common both in Byzantium and Russia as, for example, the Deesis sent from Constantinople by hegumen Athanasius to the Vysotskii-Serpukhovskii Monastery between 1387 and 1396.[30] An important panel icon of a half-length figure of Apostle Peter (Figure 13) was discovered in 1982 in London. Based on its style, the icon is attributed to the master of wall decoration in the church of St. Savior in the Chora (Kariye Camii) (Figure 14) in Constantinople. Based on the turn of the head and torso on its axis, it is logically believed to be from the Deesis Row of the sanctuary barrier.[31]

Panels of the size found in the Annunciation Cathedral in Moscow would not have been possible had it not been for the material means provided by the indigenous woodworking tradition and the abundance of available wood for panel icons in the Russian North. Russian artists like Theophanes the Greek, because of the availability of just the sort of wood types which were most suitable by means of long seasoning and gluing to make good panels, was able to expand the thematical content of the iconostasis, and give expression to its new liturgical and political meaning.

It is a generally accepted view that not only wooden churches but most stone churches as well, had a wooden iconostasis, because stone was difficult to get and stone masonry was not an indigenous artistic tradition, but one acquired from Byzantium. In the fourteenth century, with the ascendency of Moscow and renewed contact with Byzantium, stone construction once again resumed. However, the wood-working tradition of this northern region asserted itself with new impact and found its expression in the enlargement of the individual panels within the iconostasis.

Moscow artists were predominantly icon panel painters rather than fresco painters, having developed in the tradition of the (Zaleskoi Rusi) forest region, which had predominantly wooden architecture.[32] Interiors of wooden churches were not condusive to fresco technique; therefore, the more practical panels of wood increased in number and size to fulfill the pictorial requirements of the churches. The transference of the decorative program of the various architectural parts of the church interior was the result of the limitations that wooden architecture imposed on the established interior program of the church. The interior of wooden churches did not easily lend itself to wall painting and demanded, by the conditions of its materials, a substitute for wall painting. Out of necessity the established system of wall painting intended originally for stone construction had to be transposed onto individual panels and affixed in kiots on walls or onto the iconostasis.

Social, religious, and political causes are significant for determining the time at which the Russian sanctuary barrier was transformed into a completely closed wall behind which the major part of the liturgy is performed. The effectiveness of icons in prayer, their usefulness for the exposition of the liturgy, the appearance character of the liturgy from the fourteenth century on, and the wood-working tradition in Russia led to an increase in the production of icons and their subsequent inclusion into the iconostasis. The lateral and vertical expansion of the wooden iconostasis also coincides with the emerging political power of Moscow grand princes at the beginning of the fifteenth century. The effect of specifically royal patronage of art promoting the emerging image of Muscovite authority is reflected in the Deesis Row of the Annunciation Cathedral iconostasis by Theophanes.

The transformation of the open to the closed sanctuary barrier was the outcome of a change in orientation within the liturgy of the fourteenth century. The Early Byzantine Liturgy was markedly a liturgy of processions and differed from the one in usage since the fourteenth century, which consisted of a series of appearances made by the clergy from the iconostasis and their return back into the sanctuary.[33] The architecture of the Byzantine church was modified accordingly. The directional design of Early Byzantine basilicas focused one's attention with compelling force on the apse, the place of the celebrant, and the altar in front of him. The medieval church, with its central plan and central lighting, focused attention immediately in front of the iconostasis, the place of the medieval liturgical appearances.[34] The appearance character of the liturgy depended on alternation of concealment and revelation. Concealment and the appearance of the clergy to the faithful require a high barrier which provides the necessary conditions under which concealment and appearance are possible. With an open sanctuary, barrier concealment is impossible, since the celebrant and the activity within the sanctuary are visible throughout the service.

The fourteenth century was intricately connected to hesychast mysticism, which is the key for understanding the creative spirit and work of Theophanes the Greek. The growth in the size of icon panels and, therefore, the height of the iconostasis incorporating an expanded program of decoration was closely connected with the formulation of the Hesychast Doctrine, a monastic trend·important in fourteenth and fifteenth century Russia. By favoring contemplation and veneration of icons, hesychasm reaffirmed the effectiveness of icons in prayer and their usefulness for the exposition of the liturgy to the faithful. The monastic tendency to hide the mystery of the Eucharist from the faithful obliged them to visualize the liturgical symbolism of icons and their arrangement on the iconostasis.

Hesychasm derives its name from *hesychia* (solitude, silence) and refers to that current of spiritual life among Eastern Orthodox monks which is wholly directed toward pure contemplation and prayerful union with God through God's voluntary revelation of His "energy," the radiance of uncreated light.[35] Hesychasm had been practiced since the beginning of Orthodox Monasticism and had ben transmitted orally from master monk to his spiritual pupils. Saint Gregory of Sinaite had formulated and systematized the teaching of hesychasm in the beginning of the fourteenth century, when he realized that contemplative life was disappearing in Greek monasteries and only a few were practicing "pure prayer."[36] Saint Macarius was a monk of the Egyptian desert who, in the fourth centruy, laid the foundation for the "Jesus Prayer," an important element of hesychastic mysticism.[37] He appears as one of the first teachers on "pure, mental prayer," that is, the constant repetition of *Kyrie eleison* (Lord have mercy).[38]

During the Barlaam-Palamas controversy (1340–1351), the Calabrian monk Barlaam asserted the complete unknowability of God, while Gregory Palamas, the authorized spokesman for Athonite monasticism, defended the hesychast view that, while God is indeed unknowable, He does reveal Himself to man through uncreated light.[39] Following the negative publicity hesychasm had received as a result of a misinterpretation of its teachings by the Latinist Barlaam and his disciple Acindynus, hesychasm was formulated by Gregory Palamas into a doctrine which was fully sanctioned by a council of the Eastern Orthodox Church in 1351.[40] The theological and ascetical teachings of the hesychasts were composed by Saint Gregory in *The Triads for the Defense of the Holy Hesychasts* and *The Hagiorite Tome.*[41] Saint Gregory Palamas did not conceive the methods by which to reach perfect union with God; but, in his apologetic works on prayer, there was a systematic, psychological, and theological exposition of these methods for the first time in ascetic literature.

Hesychast monasticism centered in the monasteries on Mount Athos and reached its highest level of development in the lifetime of Saint Gregory Palamas (1296–1359). The triumph of this Athonite monastic theology in the fourteenth century resulted in domination of the Byzantine church by monastic clergy.[42] Its influence spread throughout the Byzantine commonwealth. This focus of Byzantine theology spread to Russia, where it affected a change toward a new monastic spirituality. This was prompted by the leading hesychasts in Russia, Saint Sergii of Radonezh (d. 1392), hegumen and founder of the Troitsa-Sergieva Lavra near Moscow and a series of other monasteries, and Saint Aleksei of Moscow (Metropolitan from 1354 to 1378).[43]

News of the Barlaam-Palamite controversy reached Russia in the second half of the fourteenth century from Mount Athos.[44] As early as 1328 the Nikonovskaia Chronicle for the first time mentions the Barlaam heresy.[45] Nicephoras Gregoras (d. 1360), in his commentary on "new texts" sent by the Palamites to Russia, mentions that in Moscow there were copies of the *Ispovedaniia* creed of the Athonite hesychasts dated to 1341.[46] These hesychast texts were inaugurated on equal footing with the liturgical texts of the Synodikon.[47] Epifanii the Wise, in his biography of Saint Sergii written between 1417–18, characterized the period from mid-fourteenth to the fifteenth century as *Sergievo vremia,* Saint Sergii's time.[48] This saint was responsible for the spread of monasticism in Russia. He was, at the same time, the propagator of hesychast spirituality which influenced and formed Russian culture of the fourteenth and fifteenth centuries.[49]

The hesychast spirit permeates the works of Theophanes the Greek. The gravity of his images and their particular spirituality flow out of the context of hesychasm. In 1378 he painted the frescoes in the Church of the Transfiguration (Figure 15) on Elijah Street in Novgorod for Boyar Vasilii Danilovich.[50] In the Trinity Chapel in the northwest corner of the gallery are frescoes of Saint Macarius of Egypt (Figure 16), Stylite Saints (Figure 17), and the Old Testament Trinity (Figure 18). A deep spiritual symbolism underlies the entire ensemble in its arrangement, composition, and style. The three separate Faces of the Trinity, symbolically contained within the wing span of the central figure, thus become one indivisible whole. The saints partake of uncreated light, which is the manifestation of the Glory of the Trinity. Saint Macarius of Egypt and the Stylites, pillars of prayer, appear totally transfigured by light and, as a result, have become receptacles of light. In these images Theophanes has captured the essence of hesychasm, the most intense moment of spiritual contemplation, better than in any other of his works. Through the assistance of solitude (hesychia) and constant invocation of "mental prayer," Saint Macarius and the Stylites manifest the ferment of grace and are suffused with the energy of God visible as uncreated light.

The Deesis Chin on the iconostasis at the Annunciation Cathedral in Moscow (Figure 11) contains the only other extant works by Theophanes. All of his figures are represented full-length and have a strong sense of monumentality and grave spirituality. The hesychast reference is clear in the text held by Christ, "I am the light ..." (John 13:46). There are presently nine panels displayed within the row (Figure 12b). These supplicating figures approach Christ, the Merciful Judge (Figure 19), from both sides in the following order: on His right the intercession is led by the Virgin Mary (Figure 20), followed by Archangel Michael (Figure 21), Apostle Peter (Figure 22), and Saint Basil the Great (Figure 23). The group on Christ's left is led by Saint John the Baptist (Figure 24), followed by Archangel Gabriel (Figure 25), Apostle Paul (Figure 26), and Saint John Chrysostom (Figure 27).

The appearance and development of the iconostasis at the end of the fourteenth and the beginning of the fifteenth centuries can be related to the fortunes of Moscow. The initial appearance of an iconostasis as a solid full screen composed of panel icons of monumental proportions permanently affixed onto an architectural frame coincides with the material prosperity and political growth of Moscow. The size of the iconostasis expanded with the increase in size of new stone churches and wooden ones which continued to be built.[51] As the dimensions of the sanctuary were increased in the newly built churches of the Grand Principality of

Moscow, so did the lateral and vertical expansion of the iconostasis until it reached its classic proportions of five rows.[52] The full-length figures and monumental proportions of wooden panels introduced by Theophanes the Greek and his assistants adapted the sanctuary barrier to the increased size of the churches and introduced a daring innovation to the Annunciation Cathedral with the supplication theme. In addition to its liturgical significance, the sanctuary barrier assumed a political character which set a precedent for subsequent developments. This allowed greater flexibility in iconography for the Deesis Row.

There is literary, stylistic, and archaeological evidence, however, to support a total composition of not nine, but thirteen panels, which included, among the nine panels presently displayed, an additional four panels representing Saint Demetrius (Figure 28), Saint George (Figure 29), and Stylites Saints Simeon and Daniel.[53] The seven central panels were traditional for a Byzantine Deesis and were standard in Russia by the fourteenth century.[54] The other six panels of Saints Basil the Great, John Chrysostom, Saints George and Demetrius, and Stylites Simeon and Daniel, along with Saint John the Baptist from the central group were inspired by political considerations.[55] They represent the patron saints of the legitimate heirs of the Muscovite Dynasty. The founder of the Muscovite Dynasty Daniel is represented by his patron saint Stylite Saint Daniel[56]; Yuri Danilovich (1319–1322) by Saint George[57]; Ivan Danilovich Kalita (1328–1340) by Saint John the Baptist[58]; Simeon Ivanovich (1340–1353) by Stylite Saint Simeon[59]; Ivan Ivanovich Krasnyi (1353–1359) by Saint John Chrysostom *(Zlatoust)*[60]; Dimitrii Ivanovich Donskoi (1362–1389) by Saint Demetrius of Thessalonika[61]; and Vasilii Dimitrievich (1389–1425), the one who commissioned the iconostasis, by Saint Basil the Great.[62] The Grand Princes were as much locked into the convention of behavior as their subjects; they only differed from them in their ability to exploit these conventions. The Muscovite Grand Princes decided and promoted their public image and that of their city. The iconostasis in question throws light on the effect of specifically royal patronage on art and how that patronage determined the perceptions of the public. The inclusion of the patron saints of the grand princes into the iconostasis of the chapel of the House of Moscow asserted the legitimacy of the Muscovite Dynasty.

All but the panels representing the Stylite Saints Simeon and Daniel are contemporary and have been dated to 1405. Both Lazarev[63] and Betin[64] consider, on stylistic grounds, the panels of Saint George (Figure 29) and Saint Demetrius (Figure 28) to be contemporary with the other nine. Two icons of the Stylite Simeon and Daniel painted on narrower panels measuring about ten inches were found in the Kremlin Museum.[65] They have been dated to the sixteenth century and are possibly copies of originals. The measurement of the iconostasis with the inclusion of the colonnettes within the row is about 35 feet and one inch (10.8 meters). The total length of the row of icons is about 34 feet and 9 inches (10.7 meters). This suggests that it would have been possible to fit nine panels presently within the iconostasis and the additional two panels of the Stylites. The panels of Saints George and Demetrius would then have flanked the row on the north and south walls in line with the Deesis Row.

The resistence to the inclusion of more icons began to dissolve in the fourteenth century because of hesychast piety and the spread of monasticism, which favored the contemplation and veneration of icons. The association of this development with hesychasm would inevitably place the origin of its background in Byzantium. The realization of it, however, was reached in Russia with Theophanes' assimilation of this tradition in his works and an introduction of a new flexibility in its iconography, which, in addition to its traditional liturgical symbolism of intercession, interprets the political expectations of his royal patronage.

NOTES

1. L. Uspenskii, "Vopros ikonostasa," *Messager de l'exarchat du patriarche russe en Europe occidentale* 44 (Paris, 1963): 239. Uspenskii offers a drawing of the classic form of the Russian iconostasis.

2. A. W. Epstein, "Middle Byzantine Sanctuary Barrier: Templon or Iconostasis?" *Journal of the British Archaelogical Association* 134 (1981): 1.

3. Uspenskii, "Vopros ikonostasa," 223.

4. Eusebius, *Ecclesiastical History,* bk. 2, chap. 4 (Migne, Patrologia Graeca 20, 846), trans. Joseph Deferrari, *Fathers of the Church* bk. 10 (Washington D.C.: Catholic University of America Press, 1969): 258-59.

5. C. Mango, *The Art of the Byzantine Empire, 312-1453, Sources and Documents* (Englewood Cliffs, New Jersey, 1972), pp. 87–88. From Paul Silentarius' account is clear that a change had occurred in the sanctuary barrier in the

sixth century.

6. E. Golubinskii, *Istoriia russkoi tserkvi,* 2nd ed., 2 Vols. (Moscow, 1904), Vol. 1, Chap. 5, Part 1, pp. 203-04.

7. *Ibid.,* p. 204; and Ann Wharton Epstein, "The Middle Byzantine Sanctuary Barrier," p. 22, where Epstein describes the Middle Byzantine sanctuary barrier. See also Cyril Mango, "On the History of the Templon and the Martyrion of St. Artemios at Constantinople," *Zograf* (Belgrade, 1979). The Martyrion of St. Artemios includes both a representation of Christ and a titular saint.

8. Mango, "On the History of the Templon," p. 43. Because this screen is attested to by literary sources of the "Miracles of Saint Artemios," Mango was able to formulate some idea of its original structure, decorative program, and function. The text of the Miracula extends from the reign of Maurice (582-602) to the year 659 and was set down by an eyewitness or witnesses before the death of Constans II in 668. From the architectural information gleaned from this text concerning the church of Saint John the Baptist in Oxeia, Mango proposes a reconstruction of the sanctuary barrier of the crypt of Saint Artemios.

9. Epstein, "The Middle Byzantine Sanctuary Barrier," p. 2. For a bibliography on this church see R. Janin, *Les églises et les monastères* (Paris, 1953), pp. 529 sqq., and A. van Milligen, *Byzantine Churches in Constantinople, Their History and Architecture* (New York: Harry N. Abrams, 1976), p. 243, plates 14, 45, 259-61. Despite its dilapidated condition, the Monastery of the Pantocrator bears traces of its former state. The South Church (Pantocrator) is the largest specimen of the four-column type in Constantinople. The nave measures 52 feet square and the dome 23 feet across. The columns, which measured seven feet in circumference, have been replaced by stone piers in the Turkish Baroque style. This church was remarkable for its decoration: magnificent opus sectile pavement and stained glass. For a reconstruction of the templon screen see A. H. S. Megaw, "Notes on Recent Work of the Byzantine Institute in Istanbul," *Dumbarton Oaks Papers* 17 (1963): 335–62, esp. 344.

10. Megaw, in "Notes on Recent Work of the Byzantine Institute in Istanbul," 335–62, esp. 344, has reconstructed the templon screen, for which Epstein in "The Middle Byzantine Sanctuary Barrier," p. 4, has recreated the epistyle program of decoration.

11. Epstein, "The Middle Byzantine Sanctuary Barrier," pp. 3–4.

12. Janin, in *Les églises et les monastères,* p. 531, suggests that the complex was rebuilt for use as a monastery between the years 1261 and 1265. Also see H. Hahnloser, ed., *La Pala d'Oro* (Florence, 1965). The sumptuous altarpiece of San Marco in Venice provides the evidence for the reconstruction of the figural decoration of this screen. This catalogue of the enamels of the Pala d'Oro provides a description and measurements for each of the panels. The account of the recognition of parts of the Pantocrator templon decoration in the Pala d'Oro by Patriarch Joseph of Constantinople in 1438 is given in Sylvestre Syropoulos, *Les mémoires du grand ecclésiarque de l'Eglise de Constantinople,*

Sylvestre Syropoulos sur le Concile de Florence (1438–9), ed., V. Laurent, *Concilium Florentium: documenta et scriptoria,* Series B, vol. 9 (Rome, 1971): 222 sqq., lines 11 sqq.

13. Epstein, "The Middle Byzantine Sanctuary Barrier," 24–25 and C. Walter, "The Origin of the Iconostasis," *Eastern Churches Review* 3 (1973): 257 and 263.

14. Epstein, "The Middle Byzantine Sanctuary Barrier," 13–14. For a discussion of the *proskynetaria* images of the Virgin of Tenderness to the left, and the enthroned Mother of God to the right, on the west faces of the two east piers, see P. Miljkovic-Pepek, "La fresque de la Vierge avec le Christ du pilier situé au nord de l'iconostase de Sainte Sophie a Ochrid," *Akten des XI internationalen Byzantinistenkongresses, Munich, 1958* (Munich, 1960), 388–91. For photographs see I. Nikolajevic-Stojkovic, "Contribution a l'étude de la sculpture byzantine de la Macedoine et de la Serbie," *Zbornik radova Srpska Akademiia. Nauka, Visantoloki Institut, 4* (1956), figs. 9 sqq.

15. Epstein, "The Middle Byzantine Sanctuary Barrier." 14–15. For a reconstruction of the sanctuary barrier, see N. Okunev, "Iconostase du XIIe siècle a Nerez," *Seminarium Kondakovianum,* III (1929), 5-21, pls. I and III.

16. Epstein, "The Middle Byzantine Sanctuary Barrier," 14. For reproduction of the upper fragments of the two *proskynetaria* images, see E. Diez and Otto Demus, *Byzantine Mosaics in Greece, Hosios Lucas and Daphni* (Cambridge, Mass., 1931), fig. 65.

17. E. Freshfield in "Notes on the Church of the Kalenders in Constantinople," *Archaeology,* 2nd series, 5 (1897): 431–8 contends that the fragments, as they stand, represent the remains of the twelfth-century templon screen. Epstein, in "Middle Byzantine Sanctuary Barrier, 7–8, disagrees and proposes that the fragments are a late reconstruction of reused pieces of marble. The finely carved upper cornices of the Kalenderhane Camii "frames" are fragments due to the unfinished nature of their terminations. Both pieces have been cut down to fit their present location. The similarity of its ornamental carving to that of the sepulchral monument on the north wall of the paraclession and the *proskynetaria* frames at Kariye Camii suggests they are contemporary to Kariye Camii and therefore date to the restoration of the Kalenderhane Camii to the Orthodox rite after the reestablish- ment of Byzantine control in Constantinople. The full report of the excavations and restoration of the Kalenderhane Camii carried out under the direction of C. L. Striker and K. D. Kuban should clarify the original use and reuse of their impressive marble fragments. Thomas Mathews, in *Byzantine Churches of Constantinople: A Photographic Survey* (University Park: Pennsylvania State University Press, 1976), p. 184 sqq., offers the best photographs published since the restoration of the church.

18. For the drawing of the location of the *proskynetaria* images in Fetiye Camii, refer to R. Anderson, in Hans Belting, Cyril Mango, and Doula Mouriki, *The Mosaics and Frescoes of St. Mary Pammakaristos (Fethiye Camii) at Istanbul,* ed.

Cyril Mango (Washington D.C.: Dumbarton Oaks Papers, 1978).

19. O. Hjort, "The Sculptures of the Kariye Camii," *Dumbarton Oaks Papers* 33 (1979): 199-289, esp. 232 sqq.; D. Oates, "A Summary Report on the Excavations of the Byzantine Institute in the Kariye Camii, 1957-8," *Dumbarton Oaks Papers* 14 (1960): 223-31; H. Belting, "Zur Skulptur aus der Zeit um 1300 in Konstantinopel," *Munchner Jahrbuch der bildenden Kunst,* dritte folge, 23 (1972): 63-111, esp. 75 sqq.; and A. Grabar, *Sculptures byzantines du moyen age XIe-XIVe siècle,* 2 vols. (Paris, 1976), 2:132.

20. Viktor Lazarev, *Feofan Grek i ego shkola* (Moscow: Iskusstvo, 1961), p. 88, and L. Uspenskii, "Vopros ikonostasa," *Messager de l'exarchat du patriarche russe en Europe occidentale* 44 (Paris, 1963): 233.

21. Golubinskii, *Istoriia russkoi tserkvi,* Vol. 1, Ch. 5, Pt. 1, p. 195.

22. *Ibid.,* pp. 197-98.

23. The text of the letter is reproduced in Lazarev, *Feofan Grek i ego shkola,* p. 113. The text was translated by the present author in Maria Cheremeteff, *The Transformation of the Russian Sanctuary Barrier and the Role of Theophanes the Greek,* Ph.D. Dissertation (Eugene: University of Oregon, 1987).

24. *Polnoe sobranie russkikh letopisei,* 3, p. 231; and M. Karger, "K voprosu ob istochnikakh letopisnykh zapisei o deiatel'nosti zodchego Petra i Feofana Greka," *Trudy otdela Akademii Nauk SSSR 12* (1956): 567-68, cited in Lazarev, *Feofan Grek i ego shkola,* p. 10, footnote 1. The Chronicle text referring to the decoration of the Transfiguration Church in Novgorod by Theophanes the Greek is quoted in Lazarev, *Feofan Grek i ego shkola,* p. 10. The text was translated by the present author in *The Transformation of the Russian Sanctuary Barrier,* p. 120.

25. Priselkov, *Troitskaia Letopis': rekonstruktsiia teksta* (M-L, 1950). The original Troitskaia Letopis' burned in the 1812 fire of Moscow. However, it was copied by N. M. Karamzin and was also preserved in the text of the Simenovskaia Letopis'. Mention of the Cathedral of Archangel Michael appears in Priselkov, *Troitskaia Letopis',* p. 450. The Russian text quoted in Lazarev, *Feofan Grek i ego shkola,* p. 11, has been translated by the present author in *The Transformation of the Russian Sanctuary Barrier,* p. 121. Reference to the Annunciation Cathedral is made in Priselkov, *Troitskaia Letopis',* p. 459. The Russian text quoted in Lazarev, *Feofan Grek i ego shkola,* p. 11 has been translated by the present author in *The Transformation of the Russian Sanctuary Barrier,* p. 121.

26. I. Grabar, "Feofan Grek," *Kazanskii muzeinyi vestnik 1* (1922): 3-20.

27. Lazarev, *Feofan Grek i ego shkola,* p. 86.

28. Uspenskii, "Vopros ikonostasa," p. 234.

29. *Ibid.*

30. Lazarev, *Feofan Grek i ego shkola,* p. 96; and Victor Lazarev, "Novye pamiatniki vizantiiskoi zhivopisi XIV veka, i Vysotskii Chin," *Vizantiiskii vremennik 4* (1951): 122-31.

31. Stavros Mihalaris and Robin Cormack, "A Major Discovery: The Icon of Saint Peter by the Master of the Monastery of Chora," *Exhibition Catalogue: Barbican Art Gallery* (London: Barbican Centre, 1983); and Robin Cormack, "A Major New Discovery: A Byzantine Panel of the fourteenth century," *Zygos 2* (1983).

32. Valerii Sergeev, *Rublev* (Moscow: Molodaia Gvardiia, 1981), p. 66.

33. Thomas F. Mathews, " 'Private' Liturgy in Byzantine Architecture: Toward a Reappraisal," *Cahiers archéologiques 30* (1982): 126.

34. *Ibid.*

35. Fr. Basil Krivosheine, "The Ascetic and Theological Teaching of Gregory Palamas," *Eastern Churches Quarterly 8* (1938-39): 31.

36. S. J. Hausherr, "Great Currents of Eastern Spirituality," *Eastern Churches Quarterly*, vol. 2, no. 4, p. 180, and Ivan M. Kontsevich, *Stiazhanie Dukha Sviatago* (Paris: 1952), p. 52.

37. J. Meyendorff, *St. Gregory Palamas and Orthodox Spirituality* (Boston: St. Vladimir's Seminary Press, 1974), p. 24.

38. *Ibid.*

39. *Ibid.*, pp. 88–89.

40. *Ibid.*, p. 103.

41. *Ibid.*, p. 95.

42. A. A. Vasiliev, *History of the Byzantine Empire 324–1453*, 2 vols. (Madison: University of Wisconsin Press, 1976) 2:664.

43. P. Kovalevskii, *Saint Serge et la spiritualité russe* (Paris, 1958), pp. 105–108. The main monasteries founded by Saint Sergii with abbots assigned to them from the Troitsa-Sergieva Lavra were: Spasskii Monastery in Moscow with Andronik as its hegumen; the Nativity of the Virgin (Simonov) Monastery near Moscow with the Saint's nephew Theodore as its hegumen; the Virgin on the Mountain on the bank of the river Nara with Afanasii as its hegumen; and a monastery in Kolomna with hegumen Gregory. Both Theodore and Athanasii had been to Constantinople, the former to accompany Bishop Dionisii of Suzdal' in 1383 and was given the title of Archimandrite. The latter was a copyist of books in the Troitsa-Sergieva Lavra. In 1401 he left for Constantinople, where he became a monk at the St. Theodore Stoudios Monastery and spent the rest of his life translating patristic and liturgical texts from Greek into Slavonic.

44. N. K. Goleizovskii, "Isikhazm i russkaia zhivopis' XIV-XV vv," *Vizantiiskii vremennik,* 29:202.

45. N. K. Goleizovskii, "Zametki o tvorchestve Feofana Greka," *Vizantiiskii vremennik* (1964), 142.

46. Nicephoras Grigoras, ed. J. P. Migne, *Patrologia Grecae,* tom 150, col. 1225–1236; and Goleizovskii, "Isikhazm i russkaia zhivopis' XIV-XV vv," 202.

47. Nathalie Labreque-Pervouchine, *L'iconostase une evolution historique en Russie*

(Montreal: Les Editions Bellarmin, 1982), pp. 61–62.

48. *Ibid.*, p. 68.

49. *Ibid.*

50. *Polnoe sobranie russkikh letopisei*, 3, p. 231.

51. M. A. Il'in, "Nekotorye predpolozheniia ob arkhitekture russkikh ikonostasov na rubezhe XIV-XV vv," *Kultura drevnei Rusi* (Moscow: Akademiia Nauk SSSR, 1966), p. 85.

52. Lazarev, *Feofan Grek i ego shkola*, p. 89.

53. N. A. Maiasova, "K istorii ikonostasa Blagoveshchenskogo Sobora Moskovskogo Kremlia," *Kultura drevnei Rusi* (Moscow: Akademiia Nauk SSSR, Institut Arkheologii, 1966), p. 154.

54. L. V. Betin, "Istoricheskie osnovy drevnerusskogo vysokogo ikonostasa," *Drevnerusskoe iskusstvo: Khudozhestvennaia kultura Moskvy i prilezhashchikh k nei kniazhestv XIV-XVI vekov* (Moscow: Nauka, 1970), p. 60.

55. *Ibid.*, pp. 60-61.

56. *Ibid.*, p. 61, and N. P. Likhachev, *Materialy dlia istorii vizantiiskoi i russkoi sfragistiki*, I (Leningrad, 1928), pp. 94-96; and M. N. Tikhomirov, *Drevniaia Moskva* (Moscow, 1947), p. 23.

57. Betin, "Istoricheskie osnovy drevnerusskogo vysokogo ikonostasa," p. 61, and A. V. Oreshnikov, "Zametki o potire Pereslavl'-Zaleskogo Sobora," *Arkheologicheskie izvestiia i zametki* (Moscow, 1897),11, 338-45.

58. Both M. N. Tikhomirov, *Srednevekovaia Moskva v XIV-XV vekov* (Moscow, 1957), p. 127, and B. A. Rybakov, *Russkie datirovannye nadpisi. Svod arkheologicheskikh istochnikov E-44* (Moscow, 1964), p. 42, consider John Climacus to be the patron saint of Ivan Danilovich Kalita. However, Betin in "Istoricheskie osnovy drevnerusskogo vysokogo ikonostasa," p. 61, has identified his patron saint as John the Baptist based on the iconography of an image on a seal attached to Ivan Kalita's deed or *gramota*.

59. On the seal attached to a religious deed (*gramota*) of Simeon the Proud is a representation of a standing saint with a cross in his hand with the inscription СЕМЕНЪ СТЪ The generally accepted identification of this saint is the one by A. V. Oreshnikov, *Materialy po istorii russkoi sfragistiki* (Moscow, 1903), p. 16, who interpreted the iconography on this seal as the martyr Simeon the Persian. However, Betin, in "Istoricheskie osnovy drevnerusskogo vysokogo ikonostasa," pp. 61-62, has identified the saint as Stylite St. Symeon and the inscription as the first two-letter abbreviation for "stylite" (*stolpnik*), (СТ) ОЛПНИКЪ.

60. The inscription on Ivan Ivanovich Krasnyi's seal appears as "agios Ivan" and has been identified as John Sviatitel' of Jerusalem, who is celebrated by the church on the same day with John Climacus, according to Oreshnikov in *Materialy po istorii russkoi sfragistiki*, p. 18. Betin in "Istoricheskie osnovy drevnerusskogo

vysokogo ikonostasa," pp. 62–63, has identified the saint as St. John Chrysostom for historical reasons and by the general character of the inscription, which suggests a well-known saint like St. John Chrysostom rather than a less well known one.

61. Betin, "Istoricheskie osnovy drevnerusskogo vysokogo ikonostasa," p. 63, has identified the patron saint of Dimitrii Donskoi as St. Demetrius of Thessalonika, whose feast day is celebrated on the 26th of October. Dimitrii Donskoi's birthday was October 12, 1351. *Polnoe sobranie russkikh letopisei,* tome XXV, p. 178.

62. The patron saint of Vasilii Dimitrievich (born December 30, 1371), the one who commissioned the iconostasis, was St. Basil the Great, whose feast day is celebrated the 31st of December, according to Betin, "Istoricheskie osnovy drevnerusskogo vysokogo ikonostasa," p. 63.

63. Lazarev, *Feofan Grek i ego shkola,* p. 91.

64. Betin, "Istoricheskie osnovy drevnerusskogo vysokogo ikonostasa," p. 59.

65. The Stylites *(Stolpniki)* Saints Simon and Daniel are not contemporary to the other eleven panels. Maiasova, "K istorii ikonostasa Blagoveshchenskogo Sobora Moskovskogo Kremlia," pp. 152–56, reconstructs the original display of all 13 panels and considers these Stolpniki panels exact copies of the originals on the basis of literary evidence. Betin, in "Istoricheskie osnovy drevnerusskogo vysokogo ikonostasa," p. 59, suggests these are smaller copies of the originals to make them fit within the new iconostasis.

Figure 1: Diagram of Classical Iconostasis (drawn after Uspenskii).

Figure 2: Bas relief of a barrier, base of the obelisk of Theodosius, c. 390—95 A.D. Hippodrome, Istanbul.

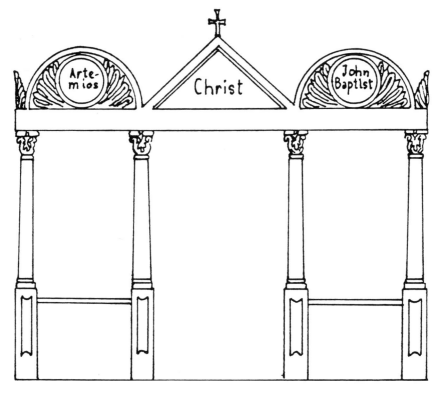

Figure 3 (above): The Martyrion of St. Artemios, reconstruction of the templon (drawn after Mango). Figure 4 (below): Pantocrator Monastery (Zeyrek Camii), Istanbul, reconstruction of the sanctuary barrier (drawn after Megaw and Epstein).

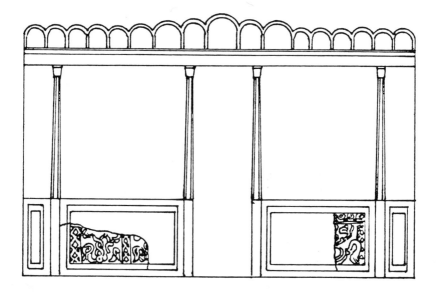

*Figure 6: St. Panteleimon, fresco icon, 12th century, St Panteleimon, Nerezi.
(See also Figure 5, next page)*

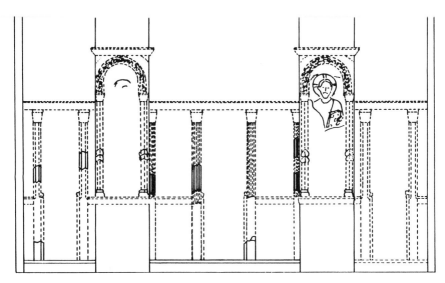

Figure 7: Katholikon of Daphni near Athens, reconstruction of the sanctuary barrier (drawn after Orlandos).

Figure 5:
Sanctuary barrier,
St. Panteleimon, Nerezi.

Figure 8: St. Mary Pammakaristos (Fetiye Camii), Istanbul, view East. Proskynetaria images on the West face of the eastern piers flanking the sanctuary (drawn after Anderson).

Figure 9: Proskynetaria image on the west face of the eastern pier flanking the sanctuary, 14th century, St. Savior in the Chora, Katholikon (Kariye Camii), Istanbul.

Figure 10: Mosaic of Christ Giving Communion to the Apostles, 12th century, Church of St. Michael, Kiev.

Figure 11: The iconostasis, Annunciation Cathedral, Kremlin, Moscow.

Figure 12: Diagram of the iconostasis (drawn after Faensen), Annunciation Cathedral, Kremlin, Moscow.

Figure 13: Apostle Peter, panel icon, possibly from the sanctuary barrier in the Church of St. Savior in the Chora (Kariye Camii) in Istanbul.

Figure 14: Anastasis fresco, 14th century, Parecclesion (Kariye Camii), Istanbul.

Figure 15 (above left): Transfiguration Church in Novgorod decorated by Theophanes the Greek in 1378.
Figure 16 (above right): Fresco of Saint Macarius of Egypt by Theophanes, 1378, Transfiguration Church, Novgorod.
Figure 17 (below left): Stylite Saints, frescoes by Theophanes, 1378, Troitskii Chapel, Transfiguration Church, Novgorod.
Figure 18 (below right): Old Testament Trinity by Theophanes, 1378, Transfiguration Church, Novgorod.

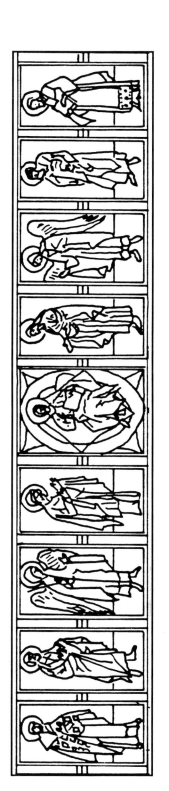

Figure 12b: Annunciation Cathedral, Moscow Kremlin, diagram of the iconastistis (drawn after Faensen) — Deesis Row.

Figure 19: Christ the Merciful Judge by Theophanes, 1405, Deesis Row, Annunication Cathedral, Kremlin, Moscow.

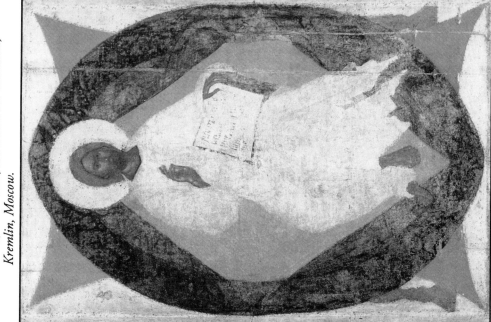

Figure 20. Virgin Mary of Theophanes, 1405, Deesis Row, Annunciation Cathedral, Kremlin, Moscow.

Figure 19. (Savior the Almighty Judge) of Theophanes, 1405, Deesis Row, Annunciation Cathedral, Kremlin, Moscow.

Figure 21. Saint John the Baptist of Theophanes, 1405, Deesis Row, Annunciation Cathedral, Kremlin, Moscow.

Figure 21: Archangel Michael by Theophanes (?), 1405, Deesis Row, Annunciation Cathedral, Kremlin, Moscow.

Figure 22: Apostle Peter by Theophanes, 1405, Deesis Row, Annunciation Cathedral, Kremlin, Moscow.

Figure 23: Saint Basil the Great by Theophanes, 1405, Deesis Row, Annunciation Cathedral, Kremlin, Moscow.

(See Figure 12b for arrangement within Deesis Row.)

Figure 25: Archangel Gabriel by Theophanes, 1405, Deesis Row, Annunciation Cathedral, Kremlin, Moscow.

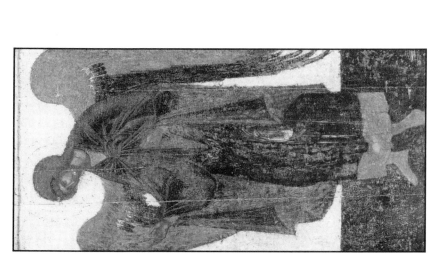

Figure 26: Apostle Paul by Theophanes, 1405, Deesis Row, Annunciation Cathedral, Kremlin, Moscow.

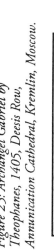

Figure 27: Saint John Chrysostom by Theophanes, 1405, Deesis Row, Annunciation Cathedral, Kremlin, Moscow.

(See Figure 12b for arrangement within Deesis Row.)

Figure 28: Saint Demetrius, 1405, Deesis Row, Annunication Cathedral, Kremlin, Moscow.

Figure 29: Saint George, 1405, Deesis Row, Annunciation Cathedral, Kremlin, Moscow.

(See Figure 12b for arrangement within Deesis Row.)

10

Political Aspects in Russian Icons

A. Dean McKenzie
University of Oregon

Although princess Ol'ga, following the death of her husband prince Igor', could be considered the first Christian ruler of Russia, it was her grandson Vladimir that became known as the baptiser of Kievan Rus'. When Grand Prince Vladimir made the far-reaching decision to adopt Eastern Christianity as the religion not only for himself but for his people in A.D. 988, the door was opened for Byzantine ecclesiastical institutions, clerics, architects, and icon painters, not to mention Byzantine politics. The fledgling Russian Church, in order to add its own saints to the lengthy martyrology imported from Constantinople, was not long in adding Russian saints to the liturgical calendar. Both Ol'ga and Vladimir were made saints while the first Russian martyrs canonized were two of the twelve sons of Vladimir, Boris and Gleb. Following the death of Vladimir in 1015 these two were among those that were murdered to consolidate the political position of their half-brother, Sviatopolk. Boris and Gleb each refused to resist his own impending execution, and, according to the accounts, they did not even allow their men to defend them. Thus, they became known as volunteer sufferers for the sake of Christ and redeemers of the Russian people. In the *Tale of Boris and Gleb* it says of them, "You have become our arms. The land of Russia has adopted you as its sword to fight against the boldness of the pagans."[1] Their canonization as Russia's first national saints took place in 1072, at which time a church was put up in their honor in Vyshegorod. Ten other Russian cities dedicated churches to Boris and Gleb. In the Novgorod Kremlin the legendary merchant Sadko built at his own expense a magnificent stone church in their honor. Icons depicting these saints from both Moscow and Novgorod dating as early as the thirteenth century are extant today (Fig. 1). It seems odd in these representations that they are frequently shown holding a sword or a spear, weapons of war, certainly not symbols of pacifism. However, the fact that their swords are shown sheathed in these early icons is a reference no doubt to their refusal to take up arms against their brother to defend their own lives. The lives of these two brothers and their canonization reflect "both Kievan politics and ... Kievan mentality." [2] In the Russian and Ukrainian churches today these saints, sometimes referred to by their christening names, Romanos and David, are still very much venerated, being celebrated six times in the liturgical year.

In the fifteenth century an unusual political theme made its appearance in the standard repertory of Novgorodian icon painting. This theme harked back 300 years to a historic battle between the cities of Novgorod and Suzdal'. It is in the *Novgorod Chronicle* that we have a record of the event.[3] The account relates that the preliminary encounter occurred when the Novgorodian force of 400 men approached Suzdal' to collect tribute. Instead of tribute the Suzdalians decided to create tribulation. Led by Andrei Bogoliubskii, they sent their military forces against the Novgorodians. The *Chronicle* tells us through typical political hyperbole that the Novgorodians managed to kill 1,300 of the 7,000 Suzdalians while losing only 15 of their own men.[4] Later in the winter of the same year Andrei Bogoliubskii sent to Novgorod his negotiatiors accompanied by a large military force. Three days of negotiation proved fruitless. On the fourth day, the *Chronicle* points out, "they came up in force, and fought all day." but the virtuous Novgorodians defeated them "by the power of the Cross, the Holy Mother of God, and the prayers of the Orthodox Archbishop Il'ia." [5]

By the fifteenth century the event took on new significance, both political and religious, especially in an elaboration by Paccomij Logofit, the Serbian writer of Vitas.[6] Paccomij emphasized that the Novgorod victory was due to celestial intervention, clearly indicating the moral superiority of the Novgorodian cause.

At least three fifteenth century examples of this theme from Novgorod icon painting have come down to us today. The three examples illustrated in Onasch's classic book[7] on icons all have three horizontal divisions (Fig. 2). In the upper tier one observes two events in Novgorod. The sacred icon of the *Virgin of the Sign (Znamenie)* is being venerated in the Church of Spaso Preobrazhenie. Clearly indicated by his vestments and a halo, Archbishop John appears with other clerics in the church. Holding the icon with him is the mayor of the city, Iakub. Then a procession is shown moving to the left across the Volkov River bridge (Fig. 3). The mayor holds aloft the icon of the Virgin followed by the Archbishop while at the front of the procession a nobleman carries the processional cross. Another welcoming procession emerges from the Novgorod Kremlin to pay their respects to the *Virgin of the Sign*. Four of them kneel and pray before the cross and icon. Clearly discernible on the left are the fortification walls of the Kremlin and the six-domed Cathedral of Holy Wisdom (Hagia Sophia), the venerated eleventh century church that still stands today.

The second tier on these Novgorod icons shows the conference between three representatives from Suzdal' and three from Novgorod. It has been pointed out that the gestures of both groups are very revealing. The Novgorodian envoys exhibit open palms in an attempt to explain and persuade. On the other hand, the Suzdalians point with their fingers suggesting menace and blame.[8] Behind the Suzdalian representatives we can see below three colorful banners a compact group of soldiers on horseback, armed to the teeth with shields, helmets, coats of mail, spears, and bows and arrows. Three of the soldiers blow trumpets as several archers let arrows fly at the Miracle-working icon of the Virgin prominently displayed like a battle standard above the fortified walls of the Novgorod Kremlin. An equally compact and regimented military force appears within the walls, some observing the proceedings from open windows. Paccomij described the multitude of Suzdalian arrows aimed at the holy icon "like a heavy rain." The legend tells that one of the arrows strikes the image of the Virgin at which she turns away from the attackers and weeps. This sacreligious act brings out the indignation of the Novgorodians. On the lowest tier they are shown charging forth on horseback from the city gate with spears and banners, determined to avenge this arrogant act of disrespect for the Holy Virgin, Mother of God. The justness of their cause is clearly indicated not only by the sword-wielding angel that attacks the Suzdalian forces, but also by the presence of four saints who lead the Novgorodian troops (Fig. 4). Three of these equestrians can be identified as the saints Boris, Gleb, and George. There is some disagreement over the identification of the fourth, the helmeted saint on the left. He could be St. Demetrius of Thessalonica,[9] Il'ia Muromets, the legendary hero of Russian folklore,[10] or Aleksandr Nevskii.[11] If Onasch's identification is correct, Aleksandr Nevskii's appearance would be anachronistic, since he lived a century later than the battle illustrated. There are compelling arguments justifying his identification as Il'ia Muromets, as was pointed out by Schaffer.[12] The presence of Boris is rather odd since, as prince of Rostov, he was also the patron saint of Suzdal'. It would raise questions about the saint's loyalty. The chronicler relates that during this battle, "some they cut down, and others they took and the rest of them escaped with difficulty." [13] We can see three bodies at the bottom of the scene of which two are decapitated soldiers. A group of Suzdalian troops has already reversed its direction and frantically retreats to the right.

That such a blatantly political theme should appear on an icon at this time has been thought to be a thinly disguised reference to the contemporary situation between Novgorod and Moscow in the fifteenth century. The Muscovites were seen as the descendants of the Suzdalians and had the same expansionist policy. The Novgorodians must have been hopeful that the twelfth century victory over the Suzdalians could be repeated with celestial assistance against the Muscovites. The following century, however, proved the futility of such wishful thinking.

The period of Ivan IV the Terrible in the sixteenth century was a particularly interesting one in the realm of architecture and icon painting. The Cathedral of St. Basil to use its most common appellation,[14] in Moscow's Red Square, has become Ivan's most well-known commission. In fact, this rather bizarre, multiple church could be thought of in a sense as an "icon" epitomizing Russia or even ironically the Soviet Union in the minds of the general public in the West.

The portrait of Ivan IV painted in an icon style, but appropriately leaving out the halo, stands at the very beginning of Russian portrait painting (Fig. 5). Ivan IV, in fact, asked a church council if portraits of living people were permitted. The church officials responded that in some cases such paintings could be permitted. It was not until the time of Peter the Great, however, that realistic portraiture independent of icon traditions became popular in Russia.

But let us turn to the most prominent political icon from the period of Ivan IV. This is an immense icon over thirteen feet long commissioned by

Ivan the Terrible to decorate his palace. The title of the icon in the eighteenth century was *"Knights Blessed by the Almighty,"* the opening of the office of vespers. The modern title, however, is perhaps more apt, *"The Church Militant"* (Fig. 6). It symbolizes Ivan's military victory over the Muslim Tatars in 1552. In that year he captured their capital at Kazan' which is symbolized by Sodom, the burning city at the far right. The victorious troops are returning home in three columns, with the cavalry in the upper and lower columns. The celestial City entitled "new Israel" seen at the far left is meant to be Holy Moscow in front of which is seated the Virgin and Child. Rows of angels descend to bring crowns of victory. The lowest column of troops is led by Aleksandr Nevskii and St. George (Fig. 7). The top column is led by Dmitri Donskoi and St. Demetrius. In the middle rank the Archangel Michael on a red horse leads the procession, followed by Ivan the Terrible dressed as a knight in shining armor carrying a red banner. Three angels above him offer a crown in what might be called the "Apotheosis of Ivan." Behind him are foot soldiers surrounding Constantine the Great[15] (Fig. 8) holding a cross, probably a reference to his famous vision before the decisive battle at the Milvian Bridge outside Rome. Behind the group of foot soldiers we see St. Vladimir and his two martyred sons, Boris and Gleb. This political icon certainly goes much further in its undisguised propaganda than the Novgorod icon discussed above.

At this point I would like to focus on the most venerated holy icon of Russian Orthodoxy, commonly called the *Vladimir Mother of God, Bogomater Vladimirskaia, Umilenie* or *Eleousa* (Fig. 9). Tradition says that this image ultimately goes back to an original painted by the Evangelist St. Luke. However, the source for so many later versions in Russian icon painting is a twelfth century Byzantine icon painted in Constantinople and sent to the Russian prince Iziaslav in Kiev.[16] Records state that Grand Duke Andrei Bogoliubskii took this icon from Vyshegorod near Kiev to his Ducal palace at Suzdal'. In 1161 the icon was set up in the Uspenskii Cathedral at Vladimir and there received a silver *riza* decorated with pearls and precious stones.

The oldest miracles attributed to the twelfth century icon date from 1163–1180s at which time it became the palladium of the region. In 1185 a great fire swept through Vladimir. The *Laurentius Chronicle* mentions that the icons in the cathedral were destroyed, but it is assumed the *Vladimir Mother of God* survived. In 1395 when Tamerlane was advancing on Moscow, Grand Prince Vasilii I mustered his troops to defend the city; but, along with Metropolitan Kiprian, he also appealed to the city of Vladimir for the loan of this miraculous icon to carry into battle. When it arrived Tamerlane suddenly withdrew to Asia without an attack. The deliverance of the city was ascribed to the presence of the holy Vladimir icon. Consequently, the Muscovites sent back to Vladimir not the original icon, but a copy by Andrei Rublev. The original twelfth century icon was set up in the Uspenskii Cathedral in the Moscow Kremlin in 1480. Today it is housed in the Tretiakov Gallery in Moscow.

In any case, this venerated image was copied many times by Russian icon painters, but the most politically oriented copy was painted by Simon Ushakov in 1668. Onasch calls Ushakov the last great master of Russian icon painting.[17] He was not only a major painter of his time, but also was involved in theoretical art discussions. Among other treatises he wrote, for example, "Words to the Lovers of Icon Painting."[18] Sometimes called a Slavic Raphael, Ushakov preferred a western style to the traditional icon style derived from Byzantine sources that had prevailed for six centuries in Russia.

As a political statement Ushakov's version of the Vladimir Mother of God leaves no doubt in the viewer's mind what heavy-handed message is meant. The title is a clear indication: *"The Vladimir Mother of God and the Planting of the Tree of Russian Domination"* (Fig. 10). In the center of a large rose bush we see Ushakov's Vladimir Virgin, a somewhat saccharine adaptation and a new type that became immensely popular in following centuries. At the base of the rose bush we see it growing within the Moscow Kremlin and out of the Cathedral of the Dormition (Fig. 11). Watering the plant to facilitate its flourishing are the Metropolitan Peter and grand Duke Ivan Danilovich. They laid the foundation stone for the cathedral in 1326. On his death bed the Metropolitan Peter prophesized to Ivan the future might of Mother Russia. Also within the Kremlin walls are represented the new family of Tsars. On the far left is Aleksei Mikhailovich and on the right is Tsarina Mar'ia Il'inichna with her children Aleksei Alekseevich and Fedor Alekseevich. The figures inclosed within the rose-bush medallions represent, on the left, secular and ecclesiastical princes of Russia and, on the right, its most famous saints. At the very top Christ appears in the clouds, ordering the angels to deliver the imperial cloak and crown to the tsar. Certainly this is one of the most blatant examples of the mixture of politics and religion. There are many other examples of this kind of mixture in Russian icon painting, but the examples we have discussed should provide sufficient evidence that Church and State were inextricably intertwined in Russia. Some of the most fascinating visual evidence of this association is found in icon painting.

NOTES

1. Constantin de Grunwald, *Saints of Russia* (New York, 1960), p. 38.
2. Nicholas Riasanovsky, *A History of Russia* (London, 1969), p. 58.
3. *The First Novgorod Chronicle in its Oldest Version (Synodal Transcript), 1016-1333/1352,* German translation and introduction by Joachim Dietze, Munich, 1971.
4. *Ibid.,* p. 67 (fol. 36).
5. *Ibid.* (fol. 37).
6. Konrad Onasch, *Icons* (New York, 1969), p. 364.
7. *Ibid.,* pp. 364–65, plates 41–43.
8. A. Anisimov, *Etiudy Novgorodskoi Ikonopisi,* "SOFIA", No. 5, Moscow, 1914, pp. 5-21.
9. V. N. Lazarev, *Novgorodian Icon-Painting* (Moscow, 1969), p. 36.
10. Natalie Schaffer, "Historic Battles on Russian Icons," *Gazette des Beaux Arts,* XXIX (1946), p. 200.
11. Onasch, *Icons,* p. 365.
12. Schaffer, "Historic Battles," p. 200. Schaffer points out that the saint is dressed like a regular Russian soldier. In icons Il'ia Muromets always is depicted in Russian armor with a helmet. Although he was never canonized, he came from a humble peasant origin to become a favorite Russian knight and was thought of as a saint and miracle worker. By the seventeenth century he was listed among the saints of Kiev.
13. *The First Novgorod Chronicle,* p. 67 (fol. 37).
14. St. Basil's, designed by the architects Barma and Posnik and originally dated 1555-60, is actually a combination of nine separate churches or chapels, each dedicated to saints and feasts celebrated on the days of Ivan's most important battles in the vicinity of Kazan'. The central tent-domed church is actually the Cathedral of the Virgin of the Intercession "by the Moat," but the entire

architectural group became known popularly by the name of Basil the Blessed, a "Holy Fool" who was famous for his outspoken criticisms of Ivan IV. See H. Faensen and V. Ivanov, *Early Russian Architecture* (New York, 1975), pp. 441-44.

15. Alpatov identifies the figure as Vladimir II Monomakh, but he is the exception. See M. V. Alpatov, *Art Treasures of Russia* (New York, 1967), p. 141.

16. For a good coverage of the political associations of this icon, see David B. Miller, "Legends of the Icon of Our Lady of Vladimir: A Study of the Development of Muscovite National Consciousness", *Speculum* (October, 1968), pp. 656-70.

17. Onasch, *Icons,* p. 132.

18. A. Voyce, *The Art and Architecture of Medieval Russia* (Norman, OK, 1967), p. 235.

Figure 1: SS Boris and Gleb, Russian icon, Moscow School, 14th century, Russian Museum, Leningrad.

*Figure 2: Battle Between the Novgorodians and the Suzdalians, Russian icon,
Novgorod School, c. 1460–70, Museum of History and Architecture, Novgorod.*

Figure 3: Battle Betwen the Novgorodians and the Suzdalians, detail: Procession across the Volkov River bridge.

Figure 4: Battle Between the Novgorodians and the Suzdalians, detail: Novgorodian troops led by military saints.

Figure 6: The Church Militant, Russian icon, Moscow School, 16th century, Tretiakov Gallery, Moscow.

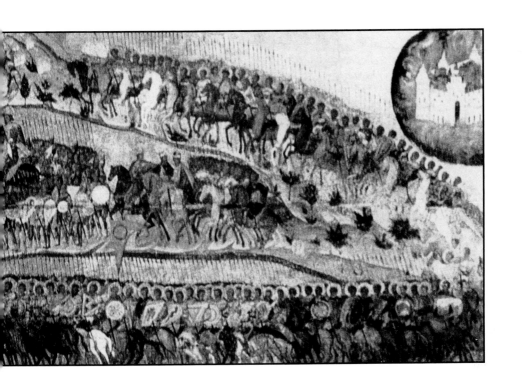

*Figure 7: The Church Militant,
detail: Saint Aleksandr Nevskii,
St. George and the saintly cavalry.*

*Figure 8: The Church Militant, detail:
Constantine the Great on horseback
surrounded by Russian foot soldiers.*

Figure 5:
Ivan IV, Russian icon, Moscow
School, 16th century, National
Museum, Copenhagen.

Figure 9:
Vladimir Mother of God (detail),
Byzantine icon, 12th century,
Tretiakov Gallery, Moscow.

Figure 10: The Vladimir Mother of God and the Planting of the Tree of Russian Domination, Russian icon by Simon Ushakov, 1668, Tretiakov Gallery, Moscow.

Figure 11: The Vladimir Mother of God and the Planting of the Tree of Russian Domination, detail: Aleksei Mikhailovich, Metropolitan Peter, grand duke Ivan Danilovich, Aleksei Alekseevich, Fedor Alekseevich and Tsarina Mar'ia Il'inichna.

Appendices

Kazan Mother of God [Russian, Moscow School, 17C.]
A.D. McKenzie Collection, Eugene, OR

A

Contributors

Maria Cheremeteff is Lecturer in art history at the California College of Arts and Crafts, Oakland. She received her Ph.D. in Art History from the University of Oregon with a dissertation on "The Transformation of the Russian Sanctuary Barrier." She was involved in an exhibition, "Holy Image, Holy Space: Icons and Frescoes from Greece," held April 1989 at the Legion of Honor Museum in San Francisco.

Basil Dmytryshyn received his Ph.D. from the University of California (Berkeley) and is Professor Emeritus of History at Portland State University. His books include: *Moscow and the Ukraine, 1918-1953* (1956); *USSR: A Concise History*, 4th edition (1984); *Imperial Russia: A Sourcebook, 1700-1917*, 2nd edition (1974); *Medieval Russia: A Sourcebook, 900-1700*, 2nd edition (1973); *Zaborona Ukrainstva 1876: The Suppression of the Ukrainian Activities in 1876* (1970); *Modernization of Russia under Peter I and Catherine II* (1974); *A History of Russia* (1977); *Russian Statecraft: The Politika of Iurii Krizhanich* (1985); *Russia's Conquest of Siberia, 1558-1700* (1985); *Russian Penetration of the North Pacific Ocean, 1700-1799* (1986); *The Soviet Union and the Middle East* (1987); *The Russian American Colonies, 1798-1867* (1989).

Josef Gulka holds Master's degrees in History and Musicology from the University of Pennsylvania, where he is presently a Teaching Fellow and Ph.D. candidate in Early Russian History. He has studied at the Curtis Institute of Music and at St. Vladimir's Orthodox Theological Seminary. A noted choral conductor, composer, transcriber, and translator of Orthodox liturgical music and texts, he is currently working on a survey of sixteenth century Russian Church Councils.

Alan Kimball is Associate Professor of modern Russian history and associate director of the symposium on "The Millennium: Christianity and Russia (A.D. 988–1988) at the University of Oregon. He received his Ph.D. from the University of Washington and was Director of the Robert D. Clark Honors College at the University of Oregon. He has also been Visiting Research Scholar at the Slavic Research Center of Hokkaido University, a fellow of the Kennan Institute for Advanced Russian Studies, and Visiting Honors Professor at the United States Naval Academy. His publications include a chapter in *Politics and Society in Provincial Russia: Saratov, 1590–1917*, and he is completing a book on the mobilization of political opposition in the Russian Empire in the middle of the nineteenth century.

Albert Leong is Associate Professor of Russian, Head of the Department of Russian, Director of the Russian and East European Studies Center, and director of the symposium on "The Millennium: Christianity and Russia (A.D. 988-1988)" at the University of Oregon, Eugene. He received his A.B., A.M., and Ph.D. from the University of Chicago and specializes in modern Russian literature, film, and culture. He has edited a special issue of *Studies in Comparative Communism* (Fall/Winter 1984-85) on "Socialist Realism: Cinema and the Arts," the *Oregon Studies in Chinese and Russian Culture (1990)*, and *The Millennium: Christianity and Russia (A.D. 988-1988)*. His book, *Space, Time, and Synthesis in Art: Essays on Art, Literature, and Philosophy by Ernst Neizvestny*, will be published in 1990 by Mosaic Press. He is currently writing a critical study, *The Art of Freedom: Ernst Neizvestny and Russian Culture.*

A. Dean McKenzie is Professor of Medieval Art History at the University of Oregon, Eugene. He received his Ph.D. from the Institute of Fine Arts, New York University. One of the few specialists on Russian icons in the United States, he has organized many icon exhibitions and published numerous catalogues of important collections and exhibitions in this country, the most recent of which is *Sacred Images and the Millennium: Christianity and Russia (A.D. 988-1988)*. He has also served as a consultant for a number of icon collections both in this country and abroad. Currently he is working on a handbook to be entitled *The Iconography of Icons.*

George P. Majeska teaches Byzantine and early Russian history at the University of Maryland. His major interest is Byzantine-Russian cultural relations. He is the author of *Russian Travelers to Constantinople in the Fourteenth and Fifteenth Centuries* (1984) and many articles on Byzantium and medieval Slavdom.

Robert L. Nichols is professor and chairman of the Department of History at Saint Olaf College. He is co-editor with Theofanis G. Stavrou of *Russian Orthodoxy under the Old Regime* (1978) and translator of George Florovsky's *Ways of Russian Theology* (2 vols., 1980-86). He is currently working on a study of modern Orthodox spirituality in the imperial period. He holds a Ph.D. in Russian history from the University of Washington.

Alexander V. Riasanovsky received his Ph.D. from Stanford University and has taught Russian history at the University of Pennsylvania for the past thirty years. He has also taught at Stanford, Harvard, Princeton, Swarthmore, Bryn Mawr, and other institutions. His areas of interest include the history of Kievan Rus' and Russian intellectual and cultural history. He is a published poet in both Russian and English.

Nicholas Valentin Riasanovsky (B.A., University of Oregon, 1943; A.M., Harvard, 1947; D.Phil., Oxon, 1949) is Sidney Hellman Ehrman Professor of European History at the University of California, Berkeley. His 250 or so publications include the following books: *Russia and the West in the Teaching of the Slavophiles* (1952); *Nicholas I and Official Nationality in Russia, 1825-1855* (1959); *A History of Russia* (1963), 4th edition (1984); *The Teaching of Charles Fourier* (1969); *A Parting of Ways: Government and the Educated Public in Russia, 1801-1855* (1976); and *The Image of Peter the Great in Russian History and Thought* (1985).

Martha Sherwood-Pike received her Ph.D. in biology from Cornell University and is Administrative Assistant in the Department of Russian and Russian and East European Center at the University of Oregon, Eugene. Among her numerous publications are articles on Soviet physicists in the collection, *The Nobel Prize: Physics.*

Donald W. Treadgold is Professor of Russian History at the University of Washington. He has written numerous books and articles, including a textbook now in its sixth edition, *Twentieth Century Russia.* In 1988 he received the AAASS award for distinguished contributions to the field of Slavic studies. He is a Fellow of the American Academy of Arts and Sciences.

William E. Watson is a graduate Fellow in the History Department of the University of Pennsylvania, and is currently writing his doctoral dissertation on medieval Arab and European intercultural contacts.

B

Catalog of Symposium Audio and Videotapes

Martha Sherwood-Pike
University of Oregon

The following is a complete listing of audio and video recordings made during the Spring 1988 symposium on "The Millennium: Christianity and Russia (A.D. 988-1988)" held at the University of Oregon. A number of these recordings correspond to articles published in this volume.

The catalog is organized as follows: entries are organized alphabetically by presenter, or by title if there is no single individual associated with the presentation. For each entry the presentor, title, University of Oregon Department of Russian tape accession number, nature of tape (AT = audiotape; VT = videotape), approximate length of presentation, and corresponding article in this volume, if any, are indicated. In cases where the title is not self-explanatory, a brief description is given. Asterisks indicate videotapes of slide-lectures or museum exhibits. These video recordings, made under poor lighting conditions, are of marginal quality. The language of all presentations (except musical performances) is English.

Duplicates of any of these tapes may be ordered at cost by calling or writing: Department of Russian, University of Oregon, Eugene, OR, 97403; telephone (503) 346-4078. Prices and ordering instructions will be sent on request. Videotapes are available only in 120-minute VHS format, and audiotapes are supplied on standard 90-minute cassettes.

AUDIO AND VIDEOTAPES

Brumfield, William C, "Photographing the Russian Empire: Prokudin-Gorsky."
(VT 172; AT 165). 45 minutes. Slide lecture giving background information on an exhibit of early twentieth-century photographs of the Russian empire housed at the Smithsonian Institute in Washington, DC. This exhibit was on display at the

University of Oregon during the symposium; VT 169 contains a survey of this display.

*Brumfield, William C "The Distinctive Character of Russian Church Architecture."

(VT 172; AT 165). 45 minutes. Slide lecture surveying the stylistic development of Russian church architecture. Photographs of Russian churches by Brumfield and A. Dean McKenzie, together with architectural models of Russian churches, were exhibited in Gallery 141 of the University of Oregon during the symposium.

*Cheremeteff, Maria, "The Development of the Russian Iconostasis."

(VT 168; AT 164). 45 minutes. Corresponds to the article, "The Transformation of the Russian Sanctuary Barrier and the Role of Theophanes the Greek," in this volume.

Christianity and Russia: Welcome.

(VT 166). 30 minutes. Opening remarks, acknowledgements, and introduction of university personnel involved in the symposium.

Christianity and Russian Culture (Forum)

(VT 175; AT 168). 90 minutes. Panel discussion with Albert Leong and Alan Kimball. Corresponds in part to preface and introduction in this volume.

Crummey, Robert O., "New Insights on Old Beliefs."

(VT 174; AT 167). 45 minutes. A discussion of the Russian Old Believer religious sect, which split off from the main body of the Russian Orthodox Church in the seventeenth century.

Gulka, Josef. "Christianity and Russian Music."

(VT 170; AT 162). 120 minutes. A lecture on Russian liturgical music with examples sung by the Kyril-Methodios Ensemble of Philadelphia. Corresponds in part to the article, "Problems of Liturgical Abuse in Sixteenth-Seventeenth Century Russia," by Gulka and Alexander Riasanovsky in this volume.

Gulka, Joseph, and the Kyril-Methodios Ensemble. "Concert of Russian Liturgical Music."

(VT 171). 120 minutes. Each piece is introduced with a brief commentary on its historical and liturgical background.

*Icon Exhibit: "Sacred Images and the Millennium."

(VT 168). 20 minutes. Visual survey of exhibition of Russian icons curated by A. Dean McKenzie and displayed at the University of Oregon Museum of Art during the symposium.

McKenzie, A. Dean. "The Meaning of Russian Icons."
(VT 167). 45 minutes. Lecture delivered in conjunction with the opening of the exhibition of Russian icons at the University of Oregon Museum of Art.

McKenzie, A. Dean. "Political Aspects in Russian Icons."
(VT 168; AT 164). 45 minutes. Corresponds to the article of the same title in this volume.

Majeska, George. "Russia: The Christian Beginnings."
(VT 169; AT 166). 45 minutes. Corresponds to the article of the same title in this volume.

Nichols, Robert L. "Prophecy and Conformity in the Russian Orthodox Church, 1943-1988."
(VT 173; AT 170). 45 minutes. Corresponds to the article of the same title in this volume.

Prokudin-Gorsky Photographic Exhibit.
(VT 169). 20 minutes. Visual survey of photographs of the Russian Empire displayed at the University of Oregon Museum of Art during the Millennium symposium.

Saint Nicholas Ensemble. "Orthodox Liturgical Music for Easter."
(VT 167). 45 minutes. Concert by choir from St. Nicholas Church (Portland, Oregon); commentary by director Dennis Oliver.

Riasanovsky, Alexander V. "Church and State: The Abolition of the Russian Patriarchate."
(VT 174; AT 163). 45 minutes. Lecture on the relationship of Church and State in Russia and the abolition of the Russian Patriarchate by Peter the Great.

Riasanovsky, Nicholas V. "The Christianization of Russia in Historical Perspective."
(VT 166). 45 minutes. Corresponds to the article of the same title in this volume.

Treadgold, Donald W. "Christianity and Russia in the Modern Era."
(VT 173; AT 170). 45 minutes. Corresponds to the article of the same name in this volume.

Watson, William E. "Islamic Perceptions of Russia's Christian Conversion."
(VT 169; AT 166). 45 minutes. Corresponds to the article of the same name in this volume.

Index